Harvard Publications in Music, 9

THE OPERAS OF ALESSANDRO SCARLATTI
Donald Jay Grout, General Editor
Volume IV

Beginning of Gerina's aria "Vi son certe damigelle" (Number 11).
Copyright Bibliothèque royale Albert Ier, Bruxelles, Manuscrits
II.3966, ff. 17'–18.

THE OPERAS OF ALESSANDRO SCARLATTI

Volume IV

THE FAITHFUL PRINCESS

Edited by Donald Jay Grout

Harvard University Press
Cambridge, Massachusetts
and London, England
1977

Publication of this book has been aided by a grant from
the Hull Memorial Publication Fund of Cornell University

Library of Congress Cataloging in Publication Data

Scarlatti, Alessandro, 1660–1725.
    [La principessa fedele]
    The faithful princess.

    (The Operas of Alessandro Scarlatti; v. 4) (Harvard
publications in music; 9)
    Italian words.
    Libretto probably by D. A. Parrino, based on an ear-
lier libretto by A. Piovene.
    Includes an English translation of the libretto by
R. A. Hall.
    1. Operas—To 1800-Scores.   I. Grout, Donald Jay.
II. Parrino, Domenico Antonio. La principessa fedele.
III. Title.   IV. Series: Harvard publications in
music; 9.
M1500.S28P64 782.1'54 70–188973
ISBN 0–674–64030–6

Acknowledgments

I wish to thank officials of the Santini Collection at the Bibliothek des bischöflichen Priesterseminars in Münster and of the Royal Library at Brussels for
permission to make use of manuscripts in their keeping for preparation of the
present edition of *The Faithful Princess*. My thanks also go to Professor Robert
A. Hall, Jr., of Cornell University for his translation of the libretto and to Miss
Michelle Fillion for assistance in preparation of the score.

"Cloudbank"
Spafford, New York

D.J.G.

Contents

Critical Notes are available from the Isham Memorial Library, Department of
Music, Harvard University

INTRODUCTION

The Story of the Faithful Princess

Among the many suitors for the hand of Cunegonda, Crown Princess of Bohemia, the chosen one was Ridolfo, Prince of Germany. But just before the nuptials were to be celebrated, and before even having seen his royal bride (knowing her only by her pictures), the unfortunate prince, on an expedition to the Holy Land, was captured and enslaved by the sultan of Egypt. At this distressing news, and moved by the thought of her plighted faith, Cunegonda resolved to go to Africa with a few small ships and attempt to rescue her beloved fiancé; but a furious tempest wrecked the ships on the very coast of Egypt. Cast ashore by the storm, Cunegonda, dressed in man's clothes, in which she had set out in order to conceal her sex and rank, was seized by Egyptian soldiers and brought before the sultan. He was pleased with the appearance and demeanor of the supposed young man, and Cunegonda, by her skill in playing and singing, so captivated that barbarian that she eventually found opportunity to rescue her promised husband and escape with him.

Such in outline was the plot of *The Faithful Princess* (*La Principessa fedele*) in the original version by Agostino Piovene which had been staged at Venice in the autumn of 1709 with music by C. F. Gasparini. The anonymous arranger[1] of the libretto for Scarlatti at Naples in the following year added to the cast a pair of comic servants, giving them several long scenes to themselves and also allowing them to intervene at many opportune (and inopportune) moments in the principal action. This, he explains, was in accordance with the "custom of this city": it was notorious at this time that no opera could succeed at Naples if it lacked comic scenes. The comic roles were sung by the contralto Santa Marchesini (Gerina) and the basso Giambattista Cavana (Mustafà), both of whom were among the most celebrated singers of Italy. Cavana had sung the comic role of Alfeo in *Eraclea* at Naples in 1700. Both he and Marchesina had already appeared many times in such roles in Venice, Naples, and other Italian cities.[2] With these two stars in the cast it was only natural that the comic element in the Naples production of *The Faithful Princess* should be more conspicuous than was usual even in that city.

Another addition to the Naples libretto affected the ending of the opera. In the Venice version Cunegonda and Ridolfo escaped without the sultan's knowledge. At Naples, it was perhaps thought politic to close the performances with a graceful tribute—or a wishful hint—to the reigning viceroy. A final scene was added so as to enable the sultan to display himself in the character of the "magnanimous ruler,"

1. Probably Domenico Antonio Parrino (1642–1716), Neapolitan editor, publisher, bookseller, and former actor; see U. Prota-Giurleo, *I teatri di Napoli nel '600* (Naples, 1962), chap. 13.
2. T. Wiel, *I teatri musicali veneziani nel settecento* (1897); P. Florimo, *Scuola musicale di Napoli*, IV (1881); B. Croce, *I teatri di Napoli* (Bari, 1916), pp. 124, 125, 134, 152.

bringing about by his own generous intervention the indispensable *lieto fine,* the happy ending.

The theme of the heroic wife had been common in both folklore and literature long before Scarlatti; to modern opera-goers it is familiar from Beethoven's *Fidelio.* The oriental setting was more of a novelty in 1710, though there had been a few earlier examples in opera and were to be many more after 1720 and especially after 1740. The best known of these is Mozart's *Entführung aus dem Serail* which, like *The Faithful Princess,* combines the rescue motive with the oriental scene in a plot enlivened by touches of comedy.

Two scenes in Scarlatti's opera—scenes which appear in both the Venice and the Naples librettos—may seem hardly necessary to the plot. One (Act I, scene xiv) is the staged combat "with unequal arms" ending in the slaughter of two of the unfortunate Mamelukes. In the other (Act III, scene v), Ridolfo is bound to a tree to serve as a helpless target for the sport of shooting with arrows. Doubtless the main purpose of both these episodes was simply to add a *frisson d'horreur* to the proceedings, but they incidentally have some dramatic justification in working up the extreme tension necessary as background for the scene immediately following in each case.

The first performance of *The Faithful Princess* took place at the Teatro San Bartolomeo in Naples on February 8, 1710. There seems to have been some local complaint around this time of the alleged difficulties of Scarlatti's music; it was said to be "too contrapuntal" and therefore above the heads of theater audiences, most of whom would have preferred "cheerful stuff and lively dances like they do at Venice."[3] Such criticism apparently had little or no effect on Scarlatti's subsequent career in Naples, for at least eight new operas of his were produced there within the next nine years. Three of these are among his most famous works: *Tigrane* (1715), *Il trionfo dell'onore* (1718), and *Cambise* (1719). There is no record of Scarlatti's *The Faithful Princess* having been taken up at any other city, but such a limited run was not unusual in a time when the production of operas was mainly a local industry and when patrons and public demanded new works every season rather than revivals of old ones, as is the case today. Moreover, Scarlatti's music was becoming less popular than it had been in the 1690s; of all his sixteen known operas from 1710 onward, only two are known ever to have made their way relatively intact to other stages. Piovene's libretto for *The Faithful Princess,* with the usual alterations and additions and with music by unnamed composers, served for operas at Genoa in 1713, Messina in 1716, and Mantua in 1718; its last recorded appearance was at Venice in 1726, under the title *Cunegonda,* with music by Antonio Vivaldi.

Sources

The known sources for Scarlatti's *The Faithful Princess* comprise one printed libretto and two manuscript orchestral scores.

Libretto *L:* La/PRINCIPESSA/FEDELE/Drama per Musica/Da rappresentarsi nel Teato di S. Barto/lomeo per il Carnivale del-/l'Anno 1710./Dedicato/All'Eminentissimo e Reverendissimo Signore/Il Signor/CARDINAL GRIMANI/Vice-Rè, Luogotenente, e Capitan Gene-/rale in questo Regno./[Emblem]/In Napoli 1710.

---

3. "Roba allegra e saltarelli come fanno a Venezia"; see L. Frati, "Un impresario teatrale del settecento e la sua biblioteca," *Rivista musicale italiana,* 18 (1911), 69.

Presso Dom. Ant. Parrino/e Michele-Luigi Muzio//Fols./ii–iv: Dedicatory epistle, Argomento, notice to the "Amico Lettore," cast of characters, and mention of "Alessandro Scarlatti Maestro della Real Capella" as composer; 92 pages, with erroneous omission of 66–73 in the numeration. Scene xv of Act I begins with Cunegoda's "Ah, nome infausto" (Number 32, measure 27, of the present edition) instead of with Gerina's entrance at "Sono arrivata a tempo" (Number 33).

Scores

Sa: Münster, Bibliothek des bischöflichen Priesterseminars, Santini Hs. 3953: 60 folios, with one unnumbered folio between 42 and 43; 18 arias, 3 duets, 1 quartet, all in full score and in the same order (except for Number 21) as in *L*, *Br*, and the present edition. The duet "Vivi O cara" (Number 96) is found only in *Sa*. A peculiar feature of this manuscript is the heading of the vocal line in each number with the name of the singer in the original cast instead of the name of the personage in the opera as was customary.

Br: Brussels, Bibliothèque Royale de Belgique II. 3966 (olim Fétis 2523): 179 folios, with one unnumbered folio between 88 and 89; full score with lacunae as follows.

Act I, scenes xiii–xiv: one page or more is lacking after fol. 47ᵛ; the missing portion includes measures 72–76 of Number 31 (supplied for this edition from *Sa*) and the first ten lines of the recitative at the beginning of scene xiv.

Act I, scene xix: in Number 40, ten lines of recitative are missing after measure 28; also lacking at this place are an aria for Mustafà, "Mira, che grazia," and seven lines of the following recitative. *Br* resumes (fol. 61) with Gerina's aria "Quel visino," Number 41; the (modern) pagination here in *Br* is continuous. The missing portion adds nothing to the plot but only prolongs the quarrel of the two *buffo* characters; possibly it was composed and then deleted before *Br* was copied. As we now have the scene, Gerina breaks in with her aria after Mustafà's question, as if in abrupt and impatient interruption.

Act III, scenes v–vi: the last fifteen lines of the recitative Number 93 are lacking; also the whole of scene vi up to "Egli mi muove" (Number 94). Here in *Br* (fol. 143) an awkward connection has been made, in a different hand, to lead into the quartet Number 95, where the original hand resumes.

Also in Act III, all of scenes vii and viii are lacking, as well as the first part of scene ix up to the recitative Number 97. With the exception of the duet in scene viii, "Vivi O caro" (Number 96), which is in *Sa*, the material missing in *Br* for these three scenes consists only of recitative.

Br also lacks all but the last three lines of recitative (Number 103) in scene x of Act III. Lacking in scene xii are an aria for Mustafà, "Sol tu sei, bella Gerina," and eighteen lines of recitative. (The remaining lines of recitative are in Number 107 of the present edition, measures 57–65.) There is no evidence in *Br* that the copyist ever had music for these portions of scene xii before him. Either Scarlatti never composed them or, more probably (since they are not virgolated[4] in the libretto), if he did compose them they were deleted at some early point, perhaps even before the first performance. They are quite superfluous, being only another

---

4. It was customary in the Italian printed librettos of this period to "virgolate" (mark with a double comma at the beginning) those lines which were not intended to be set to music. The lack of virgolation at this place in scene xii suggests that the omission had been decided upon only after the libretto was printed, thus very shortly before the premiere or even (probably soon) after it.

rather tiresome prolongation of a quarrel between the two comic characters. Since Marchesini and Cavana had already been somewhat overly conspicuous in this opera, it is conjecturable that jealousy on the part of their colleagues may have had something to do with a decision to shorten their final big scene.

The Present Edition

This edition reproduces the text of the libretto of 1710, correcting obvious errors and regularizing the spelling, punctuation, and capitalization to accord with modern Italian usage. The score is based on a conflation of *Br* and *Sa* for the numbers which these two sources have in common (Numbers 2, 9, 21, 24, 27, 31, 37, 39, 46, 50, 57, 59, 65, 69, 75, 81, 85, 92, 95, 110, and 112), on *Sa* for Number 96 (which is found only in this manuscript), and on *Br* for the remaining numbers. Key signatures as in the sources have been retained, with added accidentals where necessary to interpret the scribes' intentions. Specification of instruments and indications for tempo and dynamics when in italics are editorial, as are the few continuo figures and added accidentals in parentheses. A tie with two strokes, ⊬ , in the continuo of recitatives signifies places where in the source a measure has been divided at the end of a line. Ties with one stroke, ⊬ , are editorial, as are likewise the bracketed meter signatures (mostly in recitatives). The superfluous C, common in the sources before signatures of 3/8, 3/4, and 12/8, has been removed. There is no C in *Br* before the triple meter signatures of Numbers 100, 106, and 114. Number 37 has C 12/8 in *Br* and C 3/8 in *Sa*. Number 108 is marked C in *Br* but is notated throughout as if the signature were 12/8.

Somewhat more problematic for the interpretation of rhythm are those numbers having a signature of C with prevailing triple division of the beat: Numbers 1 (first movement), 14, 35, 39, 87, 108, and 112. All these except 39 and 112 are in *Br* only. All have been transcribed for this edition in 12/8,[5] with an occasional duplet where appropriate; the only exception is measures 8–12 of Number 11, where the contrast of duple with triple beat division seemed appropriate to both music and text at this point. (See reproduction of the relevant pages from *Br* in the frontispiece of the present edition.)

Sa has tempo indications where *Br* has none for numbers 27, 37, 46,[6] 69, 75, and 110; the *Presto* of Number 85 is found in *Br* only. The sources agree in tempo indications for Numbers 9, 57, 59, 81, and 112; elsewhere they differ as shown in the following table:

Number	Br	Sa
2	*Andante*	*Andante lento*
21	*Allegro*	*Andante*
24	*Andante*	*Moderato*
31	*Allegro*	*Prestissimo*
39	*Allegro*	*Allegrissimo*
50	*Andante*	*Andante lento*
65	*Allegro*	*Allegro assai*
92	*Allegro*	*Prestissimo*
95	*Allegro*	*Andante*

5. For a table of equivalences in this interpretation see the Introduction to *Eraclea* (Vol. I of this series), p. 10.

6. This number in *Sa* is in a different hand from that of the rest of the manuscript.

I have preferred *Sa* for this edition in all the above cases except for Number 24. In Number 29 I have changed the "All°" of *Br* to *Allegro molto* and in Number 52 combined two different indications in *Br* (*Andante* above the continuo staff, *Lento* under the violins staff). In Number 110 the note values have been halved and the signature changed from C to 2/4.

For further details concerning interpretation of the sources, variant readings, and so forth, see the Critical Notes.

The Music

Scarlatti's musical style in *The Faithful Princess* marks a stage somewhere between that of his Neapolitan productions of the late 1690s and early 1700s and that of his last operas for Rome in the years 1718 to 1721. The general formal outline, of course, is that of alternating recitatives and arias. However, this scheme had not yet reached the degree of rigidity which was to become more apparent by 1721 in *Griselda* and which soon after, under the influence of Metastasio, came to dominate Italian *opera seria*, persisting until after the middle of the century. Not every scene in *The Faithful Princess*, for example, ends with an aria, and there are numerous instances of arias at the beginning or in the middle of a scene. Especially notable are the arias at the opening of each act. These are all in simple, intimate style; two of them moreover (Numbers 44 and 82) are in the form of a "cavatina," bisectional without *da capo*. Omission of the usual *da capo* at the end of the duet Number 114, if not merely an error in the manuscript, was probably due to the need for speeding up the action here just before the final scene.

One old-fashioned feature of this opera is the presence of "continuo" arias, that is, arias accompanied simply by the harpsichord and probably one violoncello, the orchestra intervening if at all only at the ritornellos. This type of accompaniment was common in seventeenth-century Italian opera, but it was distinctly going out of favor in the early eighteenth century and by 1720 had practically disappeared. Scarlatti shows some tendency to employ it here for arias of pathos in situations of loneliness, as in Numbers 21, 89, and 98.

The usual accompaniment, however, is orchestral, with the strings in various combinations. One characteristic texture is three-part: violins in unison, voice, and basso continuo. This combination is especially frequent in the comic arias and duets of *The Faithful Princess*, but it occurs also in serious arias of vehement, energetic expression, such as Aladino's arrogant "Se si placano gli Dei" (Number 110), Ernesto's warlike "Contro l'Egitto" (Number 102), and others in major keys with fast tempo.

Notes on Performance Practice

Recitatives should be fast, lively, realistic, and varied, without marked pauses at the V-I cadences; the concluding chords at such cadences are to be played as a rule with the last notes of the voice, not after them. The voice line in arias, especially those in slow tempo, should be suitably ornamented.[7] *Notes inégales* are in order in Number 2 and probably (with discretion) in the voice part of Number

---

7. For suggestions as to the style of such ornaments see Volume I of this series, p. 13, and Volume II, p. 242.

87. Dotted notes in Number 46 may be slightly prolonged, almost as if double-dotted.

Dynamic indications in the orchestral parts, which in the sources are often found only under the first violin staff, apply to all the instruments. The general rule is that the orchestra plays *forte* at introductions and ritornellos and *piano* when accompanying the voice. Bassoons may be added to the continuo and oboes to the violins in *forte* passages. Double basses should play in all the orchestrally accompanied recitatives.

Tempo indications are to be understood more nearly according to the literal meaning of the Italian words than to the conventional sense which those words have acquired in musical usage since the eighteenth century. Thus *allegro* is bright, cheerful, or energetic, but not always or necessarily fast; similarly, *andante* means simply going or moving, sometimes (though not always) with implication of a moderate walking pace. There are some suggestive contrasts between the two source manuscripts with respect to tempo designations. *Sa* was apparently a "presentation" copy;[8] it is carefully written, with considerably more detail and fewer errors than *Br*. The latter more closely resembles the presumed original version for the Naples performances, where the composer himself presided and could indicate his intentions without always writing them in the score.

At the original performance the soprano roles of Rosana and Ernesto were sung by women, that of Ridolfo by a castrato; the alto Cunegonda was sung by a woman, the alto Arsace by a man. No violence will be done to the ideal of historical authenticity if in a modern performance all the soprano and alto roles are taken by women singers.

8. It is doubtful that any of *Sa* is in Scarlatti's own hand, as Edward J. Dent suggests in *Alessandro Scarlatti: His Life and Works* (rpt. London, 1960), p. 209.

THE FAITHFUL PRINCESS

Cast of Characters

Aladino, Sultan of Egypt	Tenor
Rosana, his reigning favorite	Soprano
Ridolfo, Prince of Germany and a captive in Egypt	Soprano
Cunegonda, Princess of Bohemia, betrothed to Ridolfo, in the garb of a man, under the name of Ersindo	Alto
Arsace, military general of the sultan, and Rosana's brother	Alto
Ernesto, admiral of Cunegonda's fleet, and Ridolfo's confidant	Soprano
Gerina, Rosana's lady-in-waiting	Contralto
Mustafà, guardian of the captives	Basso

Changes of Scene

ACT I
Shore by the mouths of the Nile, with a hut on one side
Rosana's room
Amphitheater for the slaughter of the captives, with Mamelukes

ACT II
Courtyard, connecting with the captives' prison
Royal thermal establishments, with baths

ACT III
Royal garden with tent
Room
Seashore with illuminated ships, at nighttime with the moon in the sky, and other ships around

1. Sinfonia

Segue subito

ATTO PRIMO

Scena i

Riviera sulle foci del Nilo, con capanna da cui escono Ernesto e Cunegonda.
Piccola barchetta che ha servito di trasporto ai medesimi scampati dalla tempesta, e servirà ad Ernesto per andare in ricerca delle navi.

2. *Aria*

, a-vrà pie-tà,   di me al-fin a-vrà pie-tà_____, a-vrà pie-tà.

Nè sa - rò lie-ta e be-a-ta   se con me non sia pla-ca-ta   e il mio

be - ne nè mi dà;   nè sa-rò lie - ta e be-a - ta   se con me non sia pla-ca-ta   e il mio

be-ne non mi dà, e il mio be - - ne non mi dà.

Dal segno

18

3. Recitativo

Cunegonda: An-diam.
Ernesto: No, prin-ci-pes-sa, va-da Er-ne-sto.
Cun.: Ed io so-la qui re-ste-rò sul li-do in pre-da al duo-lo?
Ern.: En-tro a quel-la ca-pan-na, e cu-sto-di-ta dal cor-te-se pa-stor che al mar ci tol-se a-vre-te più di tre-gua e men pe-ri-glio.
Cun.: Er-ne-sto, an-zi la mor-te che ve-der-mi qui so-la e ab-ban-do-na-ta. Ac-cor-da-te un in-du-gio da cui di-pen-de li-ber-tà e sa-lu-te.
Cun.: Van-ne dun-que, ma te-co ven-go-no an-cor le mie spe-ran-ze.
Ern.: E a voi re-sta-no an-co-ra ap-pres-so le mie, del re-gno e del con-sor-te i-stes-so.

4. Aria

Allegro

Violino I, II

Ernesto: Non di-spe-rar, non di-spe-rar, non di-spe-rar no, no chè il Ciel si mo-stre-rà, si mo-stre-

Continuo

rà te - co, te - co pie - to - so;

no, non di-spe-rar chè il Ciel, il Ciel si mo-stre-rà te - co pie - to -

so, il Ciel _____ te - co pie - to - so.

E pria se t'ol-trag-giò al - fin poi ti da-

rà gra - to, gra - to ri-po - so; e pria se t'ol-trag-giò al - fin poi ti da-

rà gra - to, gra - to ri-po - so, gra - to ri-po - so.

Da capo

20

Cunegonda sola

5. *Recitativo accompagnato*

Par-ti-sti, par-ti-sti Er-ne-sto ed io ri-man - go ai pian-ti. Ma se il ma-re non

eb-be pie-tà per tor-mi un' in-fe-li-ce vi-ta, que-sto bar-ba-ro li-do mi da-rà qual-che mor-te de-gna di mie sven-

tu-re e a-vrà l'E-git-to, fa-ta-le al no-stro san-gue, schia-vo Ri-dol-fo e Cu-ne-gon-da e-san-gue. Ma

Cava fuori il ritratto
di Ridolfo e l'osserva

___per be-ar-mi il co-re del mio te-sor con la vez-zo-sa i - ma-go so-spen-de-te o miei lu-mi un mo-men-to il do-lo-re.

Segue

Ri-dol-fo a-ma-to, ec-co che per se-gui-re dei tuoi bei lu-mi il rag-gio, la fe-del Cu-ne-gon-da sprez-za di ria for-tu-na o-gni em-pio ol-trag-gio.

21

Arsace, generale delle Armi del Soldano, sbarca con la
sua gente a prender acqua, gettato al lido dalla tempesta.

6. Recitativo

Cunegonda

Ma qui ar-ma-ti d'E-git-to? Ahi, son per-du-ta! Che fa-rò? Si fug-ga, si

fug-ga. Parte di voi se-gua co-lui, sol-da-ti. Quel-la stra-nie-ra spo-glia

e la fu-ga al ve-nir del no-stro Mar-te o ne-mi-co d'E-git-to o reo lo ren-de.

Ri-sto-ra-te frat-tan-to, o miei guer-rie-ri, nel-le fo-ci del Ni-lo il lab-bro ar-den-te.

Vien condotta Cunegonda
prigionera dai soldati

Gar-zon, cui diè na-tu-ra vol-to co-sì gen-til, al-le no-str'ar-mi con fug-gi-ti-vo

pie' per-chè in-vo-lar-ti? Non è stu-por se fug-ge l'a-spet-to de-gli ar-ma-ti u-no stra-nie-ro. Stra-

nie-ro? E co-me so-lo? So-no un vi-le ri-fiu-to del pas-sa-to nau-fra-gio, il no-me è Er-

sin-do, Ger-ma-nia è la mia pa-tria: ec-co in un fia-to tut-ta dei ca-si miei l'i-sto-ria ac-

22

col - ta. Ag-giun-gi a que-sti an-cor che sei mia pre - da. E - ter - ni Nu - mi! E que - sto, que-sto è dei ma - li

miei l'ul - ti-mo e il col-mo. Non ti la-gnar, chè for - se men fie-ro è il tuo de-stin del tuo ti - mo - re. For-se è de-bol scia-

gu - ra u - sci-re ap-pe - na di brac-cio a mor - te ed in-con-trar ne - i cep-pi? O - di, se ben è in-

di - spen-sa-bil leg - ge che sten-da il pie-de al - la ser-vil ca - te - na chi di nostr' ar - mi è pre - da,

al - la cor-te d'E-git - to an - zi com-pa-gno che pri-gion ver - ra - i. Scor-ta - te-lo, sol-

da - ti, al - le mie na - vi. Vie - ni, gar-zon, chè mol - to del tuo de - stin rad-dol-ci-rà il tuo vol - to.

7. *Aria*

Risoluto

Violino I

Violino II

Viola

Arsace

Continuo

Ritornello

Ma ta - lor che sem - bra in pa - ce più vi - va - ce mo-stra poi le sue ven -

det - - - - - - - - - - - - - - - te, più vi - va - ce mo - stra

poi la sue ven - det - - - - - - - - - - - - - - - - - - - te.

Dal segno

24

8. *Recitativo*

Lie-ti an-dia-mo, chè for-se vor-rà per que-sta stra-da far-si ve-der il Fa-to nel vol-to di Ri-dol-fo un dì pla-ca-to.

9. *Aria*

Ven - go,

ven-go A-mo-re o-ve m'in - vi - ta di mia sor - te qual-che lam - po di se-ren;

26

10. *Recitativo*

11. *Aria*

29

12. *Recitativo*

Gerina

Ma tempo è di chia-mar-la... O que-sta sì, ch'è bel-la! O-v'è la se-dia? O-v'è lo spec-chio, o-v'è la cas-set-ti-na, le fet-tu-ce e gli o-do-ri? Se mon-to nei fu-ro-ri, pian-ge-re vi fa-rò que-sta mat-

I paggi portano la sedia e ciò che fa di mestieri per abbellirsi Rosana

ti-na. Che raz-za ma-le-det-ta so-no i pag-gi! Pre-sto, pre-sto co-sì, po-sa, po-sa qui so-pra. Eh!

—Non si fa del be-ne se con lo-ro la sfer-za non s'a-do-pra. Ma ap-pun-to la pa-dro-na, ec-co che vie-ne.

Scena vi

Rosana e Gerina

13. *Recitativo*

Rosana

Gra-zie, poi-chè di voi so-pra il mio vol-to il re-gnan-te a-ma-tor già si com-pia-ce; rin-for-za-te gli in-can-ti on-de tra-

Gerina   Ros.

e-te pri-gio-nie-ro il suo cor di mia bel-lez-za. Ri-ve-ri-ta si-gno-ra, ve-ni-te pur chè qui già tut-to è pron-to. Mi as-si-do,

Ger.

e tu mia fi-da a-dat-ta i cri-ni col più leg-gia-dro scher-zo che può ren-der più va-go il mio sem-bian-te. La-scia-te fa-re a

Rosana canterà l'aria nel tempo
che si abbellisce al tavolino.

me, che ben sa-pe-te che son di gu-sto fi-no, sa-prò a-dat-tar-vi i nei coi na-stri e fio-ri in mo-do che il Sol-dan og-gi vi a-do-ri.

30

14. *Aria*

15. *Recitativo*

Gerina

Si-gno-ra, con li-cen-za, che que-sto ric-cio è stor-to, e poi se si con-ten-ta su que-sta guan-cia ag-giun-ger vo-glio un

neo che al Sol-dan ci-ci-sbeo fa - rà piu com-pa-rir vo-stro can-do-re, on-de per voi do-vrà mo - rir d'a-mo-re.

Scena vii
Mustafà e detti

16. *Recitativo*

Con la mia con-su-e-ta con-fi-den-za ven-go, o si-gno-ra, a far-le ri-ve-ren-za. Che re-chi? Il Gran Sol-da-no qui vie-ne a ri-ve-rir-la. A tem-po! Pre-sto, pre-sto a-scon-de-te o-gni co-sa. Ge-ri-na... O-ra ho da fa-re, non il ve-di? Un po-co di giu-di-zio a-do-pra. Ec-co il Sol-dan. Vez-zi e lu-sin-ghe al-l'o-pra.

Scena viii
Aladino e detti

17. *Recitativo*

Mia di-let-ta? Voi qui, mio re, mio nu-me? Al ful-gor dei tuoi rai tor-no, mia bel-la. An-zi a que-sto sem-bian-te voi, che sie-te il mio sol, voi gli re-ca-te. (Che pa-ro-le me-la-te!) Ba-sta, o ca-ra, si fac-cia un bre-ve in-du-gio ai ri-sal-ti d'A-mo-re. L'al-ma sa-rà in tor-men-to. Ar-sa-ce vin-ci-to-re og-gi s'a-van-za al mio re-a-le a-spet-to. Ar-sa-ce vin-ci-tor? Fe-li-ce an-nun-zio! Fa to-sto che en-tri Ar-sa-ce. Ad av-vi-sar-lo io vo-lo.

35

Arsace, Mustafà, Cunegonda e detti

18. *Recitativo*

(Or che le pal - me il mio ger - ma - no in - ne - sta an - drem più fran - chi al tro - no.) Ec - co - lo

*qui, si - gno - re. Io re - co al re - gio pie - de, si - re, le sue an - zi - chè mie vit - to - rie. Ap - pe - na lun - ge in - te - so

il ru - mor di vo - str'ar - mi fre - nò l'or - go - glio al - tier l'A - ra - bo e il Per - sa e al - fin diè il cie - lo in pre - mio al vo - stro Ar - sa - ce del - la

sua fe - del - tà vit - to - ria e pa - ce. (E qual mai se - co por - ta gar - zon stra - nier che ha mi - le gra - zie in vol - to?)

(O quan - to è va - go! E - gli mi pia - ce mol - to.) Du - ce: del tuo ri - tor - no mi - ra il pia - cer en - tro quel

vi - so ac - col - to. (Mi - ra - te quel - la dia - vo - la in ve - de - re quel fo - ra - stier, co - me lo guar - da fis - so!)

Si - gnor, Ar - sa - ce ed io ba - cia - mo a ga - ra del re - a - le fa - vor l'or - me lu - cen - ti. Ol - tre le pal - me, o si - re, vi si

de - ve un ac - qui - sto te - stè fat - to in E - git - to. Qual sia? Que - sto gar - zo - ne, che ha nel can - to e nel

36

suon ta-len-ti ec-cel-si, d'es-ser do-no non vil de-gno di-ven-ne. Mol-to mi è ca-ro, Ar-sa-ce,

per la man che lo do-na e pel suo vol-to, ma più per lo vir-tù ch'è un mio di-let-to.

(E-gli è pu-re bel-li-no.) (Ah! Che la ge-lo-sia mi ro-de il pet-to!) Di qual no-me e qual gra-do,

di quel pa-tria è co-stui? (Non eb-be al cer-to tan-ta bel-lez-za mai l'A-fri-ca tut-ta.) Vi sia no-to da

lui. Gar-zon, ra-gio-na. M'ap-pel-lo Er-sin-do; me in-fe-li-ce ac-col-se sot-to il ger-ma-no ciel non u-mil cu-na,

che di mia stel-la l'em-pie-tà mi tol-se in un pun-to fa-tal pa-tria e for-tu-na. (Che dol-ce fa-vel-

lar!) (Pie-tà ne sen-to.) (E sem-pre so-pra quel-lo ha il guar-do in-ten-to? Or io non pos-so più.) Qual ti con-dus-se de-

sti-no a que-sti li-di? Mi diè mo-to la fa-ma d'un re sì gran-de e d'un sì va-sto im-pe-ro. (Non vuoi bas-sar que-gli oc-chi?)

(Che mal c'è nel mi-rar un fo-ra-stie-ro?) So-lo giun-ge-sti? So-lo, per-chè dei miei com-pa-gni un a-van-zo son'io del-la pro-cel-la.

37

Ma dei miei ma-li non è que-sto il som-mo. Sei pur sal-vo in E-git-to e gra-to al re; di che ti la-gni, Er-sin-do?

Di cru-del schia-vi-tù. Non hai ca-te-ne. (Dei cep-pi al-trui, e non dei miei mi dol-go.) An-zi da quel mo-men-to che

di-ven-tò mia pre-da gli die-di li-ber-tà. Glie-la con-fer-mo. Chi è na-to a dar-le al-trui non ha ca-te-ne.

Ro-sa-na, io lo de-sti-no al-l'o-nor di tua cor-te. (O me fe-li-ce!) A-vrà tra miei più ca-ri (e nel mio

co-re) gra-do u-gua-le al suo mer-to (e al suo bel vol-to.) Ad-dio Ro-sa-na, at-ten-do a far va-go l'or-ro-re del-

la vi-ci-na pu-gna il tuo bel ci-glio. Pron-ta, mio si-re, e sa-rà me-co Er-sin-do. Se-gui-mi, Ar-

sa-ce, e al-lo spet-ta-col no-to ser-va il tuo ar-ri-vo ad il-lu-strar la pom-pa. A scio-glie-re gli

schia-vi va-do in fret-ta. Ab-bi cer-vel, Ge-ri-na. In-ten-di? Ho in-te-so, ho in-te-so. Ad-dio, ca-ri-na.

Ah, se non ve-do il mio Ri-dol-fo que-sta pom-pa per me non è se non fu-ne-sta.

19. *Aria*

ri - da il nu-me, il nu-me d'A-mor.

Nel tuo vol-to di-ven-ti più va-ga la pun-ta o-mi - ci - da ch'è og-get-to d'or-ror, di - ven - ti più va-ga nel tuo

vol - to la pun-ta o-mi-ci - da ch'è og-get - - to d'or-ror.

Nel - l'a -

Dal segno

40

Rosana, Cunegonda e Gerina

20. *Recitativo*

21. *Aria*

ta - ce l'ar-dor.   Fa-vel - la, fa-

vel - la e ve-drai   che in dir le tue pe - ne il lab - bro di-vie - ne sa - lu - te del cor;   fa-

vel - la, fa-vel - la, che in dir le tue pe - ne il lab - bro di-vie - ne sa - lu - te del cor.

Da capo

22. *Recitativo*

Bel gio-vi-net-to,   se go-der vo - le - te par-la-te, par-la-te, non ta-ce-te,   e che que-sto sia ve-ro

sen-ti-te un det-to del-la mia ma-e-stra: in boc-ca chiu-sa   non c'en-trò mi-ne-stra.

Cunegonda sola

23. *Recitativo*

An-dia-mo, an-dia-mo, af-fet-ti del mio ca-ro in trac-cia, che a voi l'ad-di-te-rà la mia scia-gu-ra. Se ad in-con-trar-vi un mi-se-ro si por-ta al pa-ri o più di me, quel-lo è Ri-dol-fo. Quel Ri-dol-fo, che scel-to a re-gie noz-ze fra mol-ti gran-di e for-tu-na-ti a-mi-ci, or cer-car-lo con-vien fra gli in-fe-li-ci.

Segue Aria
con Violini

24. *Aria*

Andante moderato

44

ben.   Ma pur qual ti

tutti

bra - mo a - ver - ti vor - rei   nel co - re, nel sen;   ma pur qual ti bra - mo a - ver - ti vor-

rei   nel co - re,   nel co - re, nel sen.

Dal segno

46

Anfiteatro per l'abbattimento degli schiavi con
i Mammalucchi: luogo eminente per la corte.
Mustafà e poi Ridolfo con gli altri schiavi.

25. *Aria*

26. Recitativo

Mustafà
Vien fuori Ridolfo con gli altri schiavi e Mammalucchi

Ma sa-rà tem-po or-mai d'a-pri-re a que-sti schia-vi. Ve-ni-te, ve-ni-te pur, ve-ni-te, por-ta-te-vi da

Continuo

bra-vi, chè non si trat-ta qui di ba-ga-tel-le e se giu-di-zio a-ve-te at-ten-de-te a te-ner sa-na la pel-le.

Voi al-tri Mam-ma-luc-chi an-da-te in quel-la par-te e sap-pia-te do-mar l'ar-te con l'ar-te.

(#)

Ridolfo

Com-pa-gni, ec-co il mo-men-to in cui de-ci-de per noi il de-sti-no, o li-ber-ta-de o mor-te. Mor-te di-

rei fe-li-ce se po-tes-si to-glier-mi dal pen-sier con Cu-ne-gon-da il dub-bio di sua

fe-de. Che dub-bio? Do-po il gi-ro di due so-li sen-za un av-vi-so al-men del suo do-lo-re, d'es-ser tra-

di-to il dub-bio è già cer-tez-za. Sì, ch'e-stin-to mi cre-de o pur mi bra-ma. Cru-

del sa-rai pla-ca-ta, ec-co-mi a mor-te; ma dal mio san-gue a-spet-ta nel ta-la-mo e nel tro-no al-ta ven-det-ta.

49

27. *Aria*

so.   Quel ri -

mor-so che non vie-ne dal ru-mor di mie ca-te - ne, poi-chè u-sci - to sia di vi - ta spe-ro dar - ti dal -

l'E - li - so,   poi-chè u-sci - to sia di vi - ta spe-ro dar - ti dal - l'E-li - so.

Dal segno

52

28. *Recitativo*

Arsace
Tur-ba vi - le di schia-vi, è que-sto il gior - no d'ac-qui - star col va - lor di vo-stro brac-cio al - la

Continuo

[5]
vo-stra for-tu - na un mi-glior gra - do.
Ridolfo
Du - ce: poi-chè il de - sti - no og - gi mi sce - glie a

ter - mi - nar mie pe - ne, un pia-cer vi ri-cer - co che ne-gar è de - lit - to a-gli in-fe - li - ce.

[10]
Ars.   Rid.   Mustafà
Qual fi - a? Che mi s'ac - cor - di l'av-van - tag - gio fu-ne - sto d'en-trar pri-mo in ar-rin - go.   (Sa - rà

Ars.   [15]
bra - vo co-stui.)   Di - spe - ra - to e il pen-sie - ro quan-to in-giu-sto il tuo vo-to;   ar - bi-trar non mi

li - ce ciò ch'è po-sto in ba-lìa del-la for - tu - na: at - ten-de-te in di - spar-te il no-to se-gno che vi sfi-da al ci-

[20]
men - to,   chè del Sol-dan l'a-spet-to al - la Par - ca l'or-ror can-gia in di - let - to.

Segue Aria
con Violini

53

29. *Aria*

54

van-to del re-gio pia-cer, il van - - - - - - - - to del

re - gio pia-cer.

Que-ste fan-no il mo-nar-ca più for-te e il vas-

sal - lo più ar-di - to e guer-rier_____ , più ar-di - to, ar-di - to e guer-rier,_____ guer - rier_____

, più ar-di - to e guer-rier.

Guer - ra,

Dal segno

30. *Recitativo*

Mustafà
Com-par, fa quel ch'io di - co, tan-to non t'ar-ri -schia-re chè il per - de-re la vi - ta è un gran-de in-tri-go.

Continuo
(6) 6

5 Ridolfo
An - diam, an-diam com-pa - gni, chè la mor-te è un be - ne quan-do a trar - ci d'af-fan - ni al-fin ne vie - ne.

31. *Aria*

Prestissimo

Violino I, II

Viola

Violoncello

Ridolfo

Continuo

6

Lie -

6 6
4 3

56

lie-to in-con-tro l'a-spet-to di mor-te, ho un cor d'a-da-man-te che te-ma non ha, no

no, che te-ma non sa;

lie-to in-con-tro l'a-

spet-to di mor-te, ho un cor d'a-da-man-te che te-ma non sa, che te-

- ma, che te-ma non sa.

Nel de - sti - no di ri - gi - da sor - te quest' al - ma co - stan - te re - si - ster sa-

prà,   quest' al - ma co - stan - te re - si - - - - - - - - ster, re-

si - ster sa-prà.   Lie-

Dal segno

58

Scena xiv

Aladino, Rosana, Cunegonda, Arsace e Mustafà

32. *Recitativo*

* Opening measures lacking: see Introduction.

33. Recitativo

Cunegonda, Aladino, Rosana, Arsace e Gerina

34. Recitativo

Cunegonda
(Sal-vo Ri-dol-fo? O-gni do-lor si sgom-bri.) Er-sin-do, on-de l'am-ba-scia? (Che mai di-rò?) Si-

gno-re, ho un cor sì mol-le che u-na goc-cia di san-gue ba-sta a con-ta-mi-nar-lo. (Qua-si è si-mi-le al mi-o.) E'in-de-gna, Er-sin-do,

di vol-to si gen-ti-le al-ma co-dar-da. Più co-stan-te ti vo-glio a nuo-vi in-con-tri. For-z'è, che av-vez-zo il guar-do

ad as-sal-to mag-gior re-si-sta un gior-no. (Ma se Ri-dol-fo è in ri-schio, al-l'af-fa-no pri-mier fac-cio ri-tor-no.)

35. Aria

Allegro

Violino I, II

Aladino

Continuo

Trop-po è ti-mi-do il tuo co-re or che tor-ni in li-ber-tà

Rosana, Cunegonda, Gerina e poi Mustafà

36. *Recitativo*

Al - tra ca - gio - ne, Er - sin - do, che il con - ce - pi - to or - ror eb - be l'af - fan - no. L'in - do - vi - na - ste. E d'on - de

vien? Da a - mo - re. (Io già il sa - pea, chè me l'ha det - to il co - re.) Co - sì in - u - ma - no ti tor - men - ta l'al - ma

che ti ri - du - ca a tra - mor - tir di do - glia? La vi - sta del mio be - ne (e che vi - sta cru - del!) cau - sò l'af - fan - no. Lo ve -

de - sti, e pre - sen - te al - lo spet - ta - co - lo fu? N'a - vea gran par - te. (Al - tra don - na non vi - di.) (Quand' e - gli ven - ne me - no non

e - ro giun - to an - co - ra.) Le fa - vel - la - sti? Ah! Chè ta - cer fu for - za, e il car - ne - fi - ce fu il mio si - len - zio. (Gio - va i - nol - trar - si

più.) T'e - ra lun - gi o vi - cin? (Trop - po tra - scor - si.) Su fa - vel - la! Ah! Che in - va - no mi ten - ta - te di

più, se non lo dis - si per ti - mor del - la mor - te o - ra men lo di - rò per com - pia - cer - vi.

65

37. Aria

Quan-do poi ve-drai lo stra - le, lo stra-le che ho nel sen n'a-vrai pie - tà, n'a-vrai pie-

tà _____ , n'a-vrai pie - tà; quan - do poi ve-drai lo stra-le, lo

stra - le che ho nel sen n'a-vrai pie - tà _____ pie - tà _____ pie - tà _____

66

Rosana, Gerina e Mustafà

38. *Recitativo*

Va, va. Do-ve? Con Er-sin-do. O-ra ho che fa-re. Gli ho det-to do-ve ei mi do-vrà a-spet-ta-re! Spe-me e ti-

mo-re a chi, a chi di voi dò fe-de? Mi lu-sin-ga d'a-mor, poi con-tu-ma-ce con si-len-zio im-por-tun d'ar-mar-mi ei ta-ce.

Ma pur ch'io sia l'a-ma-ta, ben-chè il sap-pia d'al-trui, sa-rò be-a-ta.

39. *Aria*

Un' au-ra lu-sin-ghie-ra,

un' au-ra lu-sin-ghie-ra spe-ra mi di-ce, spe-ra tu, tu sei la bel-

Mustafà e Gerina

40. *Recitativo*

Zi, zi, u-na pa-ro-la. Io de-vo an-dar con la pa-dro-na mia. E vo-stra si-gno-

ria se ne va sen-za a me vol-ge-re un guar-do? Sai ben, sai ben ch'io pe-no ed ar-do,

ma d'al-lor che ve-de-sti il fi-gu-ri-no che sì, che sì, che l'in-do-vi-no, qual-che dia-vol t'è en-tra-to nel-la

te-sta. (La con-giun-tu-ra è que-sta per far-lo di-spe-rar.) Io di-co il ve-ro, ma

sia con vo-stra pa-ce as-sai, as-sai quel fo-ra-stier mi al-let-ta e pia-ce. (Po-ter del mon-do!) E co-me,

co-me po-trai ri-dur-ti a mi-rar di buon oc-chio... O que-sta si ch'è bel-la. Co-stu-me è d'o-gni don-na mi-rar con più di-

let-to il fo-ra-stie-ro che il cit-ta-din che sem-pre l'ha d'a-van-ti. Dun-que cru-del, ti van-ti di mi-rar con più gu-sto quel cor-

puc-cio me-schin che que-sto fu-sto? Si-cu-ro, si-cu-ro, e n'ho ra-gio-ne. Qual è?

(Continuation lacking
in the score: see
Introduction)

41. *Aria*

no, non mi cu-ro, no no no no no no, nè mi cu - ro più di te, no, nè mi cu - ro più di te.

Le sue lu - ci sì vi - va - ci, sì vi - va - ci son le

fa - ci che al mio co - re dan-no ar-do - re, dan-no ar-do - re ed il cor gli giu - ra fè, gli giu - ra

fè; le sue lu - ci sì vi - va - ci, sì vi - va - ci son le fa - ci che al mio co - re dan-no ar-

do - re ed il cor gli giu - ra fè, ed il cor gli giu - ra, giu - ra, gli giu - ra fè.

Da capo

42. Recitativo

43. *Duetto*

Fine del Primo Atto

Da capo

ATTO SECONDO

Scena i
Cortile corrispondente al Serraglio degli schiavi
Ernesto e poi Mustafà

44. *Aria*

45. *Recitativo*

Ernesto
In-va-no, in-van rac-col-si le spar-se na-vi in so-li-ta-rio li-do se Cu-ne-gon-da non ri-tro-vo an-co-ra.

Mustafà
(An-cor non veg-go il zer-bi-not-to Er-sin-do.) (Co-lui che al vol-to e trat-to sem-bra ser-vo di cor-te, for-se che di Ri-dol-fo a-vrà con-tez-za.) (Chi sa-rà mai co-stui?)

Ern. A-mi-co: il Ciel ti guar-di. Par-la con me vos-si-gno-ria? Ap-pun-to. A che deg-gio ser-vir-la? Non ti fia gra-ve il dir-mi se t'è no-to fra schia-vi un tal Ri-dol-fo. Ri-dol-fo? Si-cu-ris-si-mo, poi-chè di tut-ti gli schia-vi io son cu-sto-de, e que-sto tal Ri-dol-fo m'è fra tut-ti il più ca-ro. (Fe-li-ce sor-te!) A-mi-co, se a me per-met-ti il fa-vel-lar con quel-lo a-vrà de-gna mer-ce-de il tuo fa-vo-re. Scher-za lei, mio si-

gno- re;   io per fa- re un ser- vi- zio ad un par suo non vo con in- te- res- se. Pren- di.   Cos' è?   Poc'

o- ro: in pre- mio no,   ma sol del- l'o- pra tua d'un gra- to cor pic- co- lo se- gno è que- sto,

e se... Fa- vel- li pur.   E se pro- met- ti   a Ri- dol- fo dar cam- po me- co fug- gir a-

vrai quan- to bra- mar sa- prai.   Quest'è un cer- to ne- go- zio che non si può toc- car sì fa- cil-

men- te,   per- chè in E- git- to v'è u- na gran giu- sti- zia.   Qual ti- mor, se con noi po- trai fug- gi- re?   E'

ve- ro ciò, ma è d'uo- po ch'io ci pen- si: per or non gliel pro- met- to,   ma qui in- tor- no lei si trat- ten- ga   e poi per con-

dur- lo a Ri- dol- fo   in bre- ve io tor- no.   In te con- fi- do.   Ad- di- o.   O me fe- li- ce!

Ma che fia di Ri- dol- fo al- lor ch'io ren- da   del- la fe- del con- sor- te pa- le- se a lui   la per- di- ta in- fe- li- ce?

46. *Aria*

82

mor - te del mio in-gan - no si la - - - - - - - gna, si la-gna la Fè,

del mio in-gan - no si la - gna la Fè.

E se par - lo si ren - de più for - te il tor - men - to dei

lac - ci del piè, si ren - de più for - te il tor - men - - to dei lac - ci del piè.

Da capo

Mustafà e poi Cunegonda

47. *Recitativo*

48. *Aria*

49. Recitativo

Ma Er-sin -do di già vie - ne. A chi par - lar vo - le-te? Io sol de - sio Ri -

dol-fo di Ger-ma-nia. Or ve lo man-do. Se in que-sto dì la sor - te non mi ar - ri-de pie-to - sa io son di mor-te.

50. *Aria*

Andante lento

Giu - sti Nu - mi,

violoncelli soli

ma, quest' al - ma fe-del.

Chè sì fie - ro s'è

tutti

re - so il do - lo - re del - l'a - ni - ma mi - a   ch'è trop - po cru-del,   è trop - - po, è

trop - po cru-del_____, è trop-po, è trop-po cru - del.

Dal segno

88

Scena iii

Cunegonda e Ridolfo

51. *Recitativo*

89

già più d'un fo-glio. Non m'a-du-lar. Per que-sto pri-mo am-ples-so che in se-gno d'a-mi-ci-zia al sen ti sten-do, dim-mi se d'al-tri è Cu-ne-gon-da in

brac-cio. (Tu mor-rai se ciò di-co, ed io se tac-cio.) Par-la. Ah! Sì com-pren-do, è in-fe-del Cu-ne-gon-da op-pu-re è mor-ta. No, pren-ce,

ti con-for-ta: el-la e fe-del più as-sai che non la bra-mi. Qual pro-va? (Oh, che do-lor co-pri-re il ve-ro!) Se co

l'on-de sol-cai men-tre la fi-da per la tua li-ber-tà ven-ne in E-git-to. Cu-ne-gon-da in E-git-to? Al-men lo spe-ro.

Se-co tu non ve-ni-sti? Ci di-vi-se, pria che al li-do ap-pro-dar, fie-ra pro-cel-la. Ed in es-sa pe-rì? Gio-va in sal-vo spe-rar co-

tan-ta fe-de. Ah! Ch'el-la è mor-ta. Trop-po, trop-po del-la sua vi-ta il cer-to ri-schio sen-to, che più d'in-fe-del-tà mi dà tor-men-to.

52. Duetto

Andante lento

Violino I, II

Ridolfo

Tu sei mor-ta,   tu sei

Cunegonda

Continuo

mor-ta,   o don-na a-man-te   e t'uc-ci-se la tua fè, e t'uc-ci-se, t'uc-ci-se

92

53. *Recitativo*

54. *Recitativo*

55. Aria

Rosana, Ridolfo, Cunegonda, Gerina e poi Mustafà

56. *Recitativo*

da-to da guar-die e da cu-sto-di. (Quan-to di-ce è per me.)(Non v'è più dub-bio.) Che im-por-ta che sian no-ti al-la ple-be del Ni - lo

a-mor stra-nie-ri? Per-chè sta in lor po-ter l'i-do-lo mi-o. (Che più, mia fi-da? E ta-le an-cor son i-o.) (E' cer-to, si, cer-tis-si-mo.)

Que-ste di-mo-re, a-mi-co, son fo-men-to al-le bra-me del-la don-na po-ten-te e ri-so-lu-ta. Non cer-

car un se-gre-to che men-tre re-sta oc-cul-to a te non ca-le. Se non ca-le a co-stui, pre-me a Ro-sa-na. Rad-dop-pier-an-si i cep-pi a que-sto

fol-le, che non sve-la un se-gre-to, e da-ran-si a co-lui che non lo vol-le. Poi-chè a for-za si vuol, e quel-la

pe-na è pre-scrit-ta al ta-cer, che a far pa-le-se l'og-get-to del mio a-mo-re dil-le che l'ho pre-sen-te, e quel tu sa-i. (A Ro-sa-na?)

Non più, son sod-di-sfat-ta. O-là! Ec-co-mi qui. Sian con-dot-ti co-sto-ro ai re-gi Ba-gni l'un dal-l'al-tro di-vi-si.

Fa-rò quan-to im-po-ne-te. (I - vi men os-ser-va-ta e sen-za in-ciam-pi, mi fa-rò del suo a-mo-re an-cor più cer-ta.)

(Che bra-ma-te di più, si-gno-ra bel-la? Mi par che as-sai ben chia-ro e-gli fa-vel-la.)

98

57. *Aria*

99

58. *Recitativo*

59. *Duetto*

Io ri - tor - no al - le ca - te - ne,   ma pria

Tu ri - tor - ni al - le ca - te - ne,

dim - mi dov'è il be - ne del mio cor, dov' è il be - ne del mio cor;

nè dir pos - so il tuo ben son io mio cor___, son io mio cor;

io ri - tor - no al - le ca - te - ne ma pria dim - mi dov'è il be - ne, dov'è il be - ne del mio

tu ri - tor - ni al - le ca - te - ne nè dir pos - so___ il tuo ben son io, son io mio

Deh, po - tes - si, po - tes - si dir - gli al - me - no, al - me - no ch'il mio cor gli di - ce ad - di - o

Deh, po - tes - si, po - tes - si dir - gli al - me - no, al - me - no

soli

tut - to fe - de e tut - to a - mor, ad - dio

ch'il mio cor gli di - ce ad - di - o tut - to fe - de e tut - to a - mor, ad - dio

tut - to fe - de e tut - to a - mor, e tut - to, tut - to a - mor.

tut - to fe - de e tut - to a - mor, e tut - to a - mor.

tutti

6 #6   # 6 6 3
              4

Dal segno

104

Gerina e Mustafà

60. Recitativo

(Er - sin - do già si par - te: io vo' se-guir-lo per da - re a Mu - sta - fà mag-gior do -

lo - re.) Ge - ri - na, o - ve si va? Do - ve mi pia - ce: o que-sta si, ch'è bel - la! Deg-gio a te con-to

dar dei pas - si miei? Si - cu - ro, si-cu - ro, e t'ho fer-ma - ta per - chè se-gui-vi Er-sin - do. E Er - sin - do io

se - guo. Fer - ma - ti, tra-di-tri - ce; di', non sai che dis-di - ce a te che hai giu-ra - to e fe - de e a -

mo - re an - da-re ap-pres - so ad al - tri? Eh! bi - so - gno non ho di bel l'u - mo - re.

61. *Aria*

trò _____ , po-trò,   po-trò.   Non mi sgo-men-to di tue pa-

ro - le   e quan-do vo-glio co-tan-to or-go-glio do-mar___, do-mar sa-prò,   e quan-do vo-glio, quan-do vo -

glio   co-tan-to or-go-glio do-mar sa-prò, do-mar sa - prò,   sa-prò do-mar, do-mar sa - prò.

Da capo

62. Recitativo

63. Duetto

109

110

Terme con bagni.
Rosana, poi Arsace

64. *Recitativo*

Rosana
Smanie d'amor, presto, presto sarete in calma; ma quanto impaziente al-tret-tanto gelosa è mia fiamma poichè fatta palese al noto schiavo. Pria che altrui la riveli, egli si perda.

Arsace
Regina, ai cenni tuoi.

Ros.
Odimi, Arsace: quello schiavo europeo guidato al bagno dai ministri.

Ars.
Il vidi.

Ros.
Costui deve guardarsi con cauta gelosia, tanto che nasca qualche incontro opportun per dargli morte.

Ars.
Ma la perdita sua tanto rileva?

Ros.
Quanto la mia grandezza e il tuo comando. E' a parte d'un segreto che, palesato, a entrambi è un gran periglio.

Ars.
Argo il custodirà, nè dalle porte fuori uscirà che per condursi a morte.

111

65. *Aria*

rea di mor - te di - vie - ne ta-lor.

Quel - la stra - ge che un so - glio di - fen - de di giu - sti - zia rac - chiu - de il vi - gor, di giu -

sti - zia rac - chiu - de, rac - chiu - de il vi - gor_____, rac - chiu - de il vi - gor.

Dal segno

113

Rosana posta a sedere, Cunegonda sopravviene.

66. *Recitativo*

di - ta.) Vie - ni, cor mio, non ti at - ter - rir sui lam-pi di re-al ma-e-stà, che A-mor gli ha op-pres-si. (Il

suo nas-cen-te a-mor si tron-chi in cul - la.) Che tar - di, che tar-di più? Don-na, ve-der so-spi - ro

tol - to voi da un in-gan-no, e me di pe - na. Vor-rei tar-pa-ti i van - ni ad un a-mor che sen-za spe - me è

na - to. Quel lab-bro tra-di-tor dis-se d'a-mar-mi. D'a-mar-vi io dis-si mai? V'è l'in-no-

cen - te! Non di-ce-sti a Ri-dol-fo ch'il tuo be-ne è pre-sen-te? Il dis-si. V'e-ra al-tra don-na? Non

v'e - ra. E sog-giun-ge-sti po-scia ri-vol-to a me, che quel-la so-no? Con voi non fa-vel-lai. Tu

men-ti, in-de-gno. Sei reo, sei reo d'a-ver-mi a for-za d'un in-gan - no fuor del-l'in-cau-to se - no trat-to un a-

mor, che non gra-di-to, è fol - le. U-no stra-nie-ro vil...Gran-de ab-ba-stan-za ti ren-de-va il mio af-fet-to. Reo non sa-rei...

Chiu-di fel-lon quel lab-bro. Ub-bi-di-sco. Dis-col-pe non am-met-te u-na fiam-ma d'a-mor ch'è fat-ta sde-gno.

115

67. *Aria*

ful - mi - ne e sa - et - te ca-de-ran_____, ca-de-ran_____ sul tra - di -

tor, sul tra - di - tor; lam-po, ful - mi - ne e sa - et - te ca-de-ran_____

_____ sul tra - di - tor_____, sul tra - - di - tor, tra-di-tor, tra-di-

tor.

Sul - l'al-tar del-la ven-

Dal segno

118

68. Recitativo

69. Aria

tal.

Già

lan - gue tra - di - ta del sen la co - stan - za con pia - ga, con pia - ga mor-

tal;   già lan - gue tra - di - ta del sen la co - stan - za con pia - ga, con

pia - ga mor - tal_____ , con pia - ga mor - tal.

tutti

Dal segno

121

70. *Recitativo*

Arsace, Ridolfo, Ernesto

71. *Recitativo*

Ferma, in-de-gno, le pian-te. E tu, che al vol-to e al-le in-co-gni-te spo-glie te pa-le-si stra-

nier, co-me por-ta-sti fra que-ste mu-ra te-me-ra-rio il pie-de? (Che di-rò mai?) Mi

spin-se il de-sio d'am-mi-rar si va-sta mo-le. (Già di per-der co-lui na-sce l'in-con-tro.)

Chi vien am-mi-ra-tor d'a-ver non cu-ra il con-gres-so con gli schia-vi; am-bi ten-ta-ste la con-cer-ta-ta

fu-ga, e rei già sie-te. Non si trat-tan le fu-ghe tra mi-ni-stri e cu-sto-di. E' lo stra-nie-ro na-to nel-

la mia pa-tria. E più cer-to per-ciò si fa il de-lit-to. Ma qui il Sol-dan.

Sap-pia la col-pa e im-pon-ga qual si de-ve al-l'ar-dir pe-na se-ve-ra.

123

72. Recitativo

Arsace, Ridolfo, Ernesto e poi Mustafà

73. *Recitativo*

Mi se-gua lo stra-nie-ro. O - là! Si - gno - re, che chie-di? Dai sol-da - ti sia con-dot - to lo schia-vo nel giar-di - no re-a-le al-la sua pe - na. Ub-bi-di-rò i suoi cen - ni. Si - gnor, vi la-scio e mo-ri-rò con-ten - to se mi sa-rà con-ces - so coi vo-stri u-nir gli ul-ti-mi miei so - spi - ri.

74. *Recitativo accompagnato*

Cu - ne-gon-da, m'at-ten - de sul-la spon-de di Le - te o - ve t'in-vio mes-sag-ge - ro un so-spir del ve - nir mi - o.

75. *Aria*

126

giun-ger-ti a-gli E-li-si, om - bra a-do-ra - - - - - - - ta.

f tutti

(6/4) 7# 6/4 # 6/4 # 6/4 # #6 6 6 #

Ca - ra, soli

ca - ra se ti per-dei la mor-te mia tu se - i, ma del-la vi-ta più, ma del-la vi-ta più mor -

te bra-ma - ta; ca - ra, la mor-te mia tu sei, ma del-la vi-ta più mor - te bra-ma - ta.

Da capo

Mustafà e poi Gerina con uno schiavo
con sciabola e bastone in mano

76. *Recitativo*

Ancor voi lo se-gui-te al re-a-le giar-di-no; i-vi sia cu-sto-di-to e m'a-spet-ta-te.

Mu-sta-fà, Mu-sta-fà pen-sa un po-co ai tuo-i fat-ti. Qui s'ha da far con mat-ti; quel-la fol-le ra-

gaz-za po-co fa t'ha in-con-tra-to sen-za dir-ti nien-te, e un' al-tra vol-ta an-cor t'ha mi-nac-

cia-to. Che sì, che sì, che con la tua bra-vu-ra suc-ce-der ti po-trà qual-che pa-u-ra.

77. *Aria*

Allegro moderato

Violino I, II

Mustafà

O-gni fron-da che si muo-ve mi fa

Continuo

su-bi-to ap-pren-sio-ne, su-bi-to mi fa ap-pre-en-si-o-ne,

par che il co - re ed il pul-mo-ne al___ suo lo - co più non sta, par che il

co - re ed il pul-mo - ne al suo lo - - co più non sta, più non

sta. Quan-to va Mu-sta-fà che Ge-ri-na te l'ha

det - to, Ge-ri-na te l'ha det - to, te l'ha det-to e te la fa, te la fa, te la

fa, e te la fa; quan - to va Mu-sta-fà che Ge-ri-na te l'ha det-to, te l'ha

det-to e te la fa, te la fa, te la fa, e te la fa.

Da capo

129

78. *Recitativo*

of - fi - cial par mio deg - gia pas - sar per sot - to...Del ba - sto - ne, si-gnor sì; o - ra è il tem - po. (Che deg - gio

far?) Al - me - no... Non più, co - sì ha da es - se - re. A te! A - da - gio, a - da - gio...

(O me in - fe - li - ce!) So - lo la ge - lo - sia... (Cre - po di ri - so.) Mi fe' mon - tar in

col - le - ra...(Tre - ma da ca - po a piè.) Del re - sto poi sei tu... Si - len - zio in - de - gno, e non par - lar - mi più.

79. *Aria*

Suv - via, suv-via ben mi -

o, ben mi - o, ben mi - o non te - me - re, non te - me - re, mo-stra bra-vu - ra, mo-stra bra-

132

80. Recitativo

spal-la mi da un gra-ve do-lo-re. Di', di' che non hai va-lo-re. Non ho va-

Mustafà cava la sciabola, e nel volersi ponere in guardia, si ferma.

lor? Po-ter del mon-do... Ahi! Ahi! Cos' è, cos' è? C'è for-se un' al-tra scu-sa ma-gra? Ap-

pun-to or m'è ve-nu-ta la po-da-gra. Non ser-von que-ste ciar-le. Se non ti bat-ti io ti fa-rò am-maz-za-re.

Pia-no, pia-no bel bel-lo. (Che gu-sto!) (E non c'è un ca-ne che ven-ga ad im-pe-dir que-sto du-el-lo?) Al-

Segue il duello

l'ar-mi su, non c'è più che tar-da-re. Con tut-to il mio do-lor ci vo pro-va-re.

Mustafà cade e resta privo di spada.

Pie-tà, pie-tà. Do-man-da-mi la vi-ta. La vi-ta, la vi-ta in ca-ri-tà. Ti sia do-na-ta, ma im-

pa-ra un' al-tra vol-ta e fa-re il bell' u-mo-re. Più nol fa-rò. (Sia ma-le-det-to a-mo-re.) Ga-lan-tuo-mo, tu van-ne;

sa-prò, sa-prò ri-mu-ne-rar tua biz-za-ri-a. Ri-mu-ne-ra il ma-lan che il Ciel gli di-a.

134

81. Duo dei Buffi

chè non l'ho am-maz-za-to? Il tuo a - spet - to ho ri - spet - ta - to chè in ve - der co - lui mo - ri - re

ti po - te - vi tra-mor-ti - re, tan - to san-gue, tan - to san-gue in ri - mi - rar.

Ob - bli -

ga-ta del fa-vo-re, ch'io si - cu-ro ho un cer - to co - re co - sì te - ne - ro di pa-sta che un tan - tin di san-gue

ba-sta in de - li - quio a far-mi an-dar, in de - li - quio a far-mi an-dar.

Fine dell'Atto Secondo

Da capo

ATTO TERZO

Giardino reale con tenda, sotto cui dovrà sedere il Soldano.
Rosana, Gerina e poi Arsace

82. *Aria*

Andante e lento

Me - sti A - mo - ri di - sprez - za - ti, non vo'u-dir - vi la - gri - mar_____, la-gri-mar;

non vo'u-dir-vi me - sti A - mo-ri, me-sti A-mo-ri di-sprez-za - ti, non vo'u-
soli

dir - vi la-gri-mar _____ , la - - gri - mar _____

_____ , la - gri-mar.

83. *Recitativo*

Gerina: Eh! Che tan-ti la-men-ti non ci vo-glion, si-gno-ra; sva-ri-ar-si bi-so-gna e cre-da che il go-der non

Arsace: è ver-go-gna. Ro-sa-na, al tuo de-sio fau-sta è la sor-te. Nac-que l'in-con-tro già ed è vi-ci-no l'o-dia-to schia-vo a de-sti-na-ta mor-te.

Rosana: E cre-di poi con que-sta mor-te so-la a-ver po-sto in si-cu-ro a me il tro-no d'E-git-to, a te il co-man-do?

Ars. Vi ri-man qual-che in-ciam-po?

Ros. O Dei! lo te-mo. Quel gar-zo-ne stra-nier trop-po è gra-di-to.

Ars. E che può vil fan-ciul og-gi in E-git-to?

Ros. Mol-to in vo-lu-bil cor, più nel Sol-da-no.

Ars. Va-no e in-u-til pen-sie-ro.

Ger. Il Sol-da-no ed Er-sin-do son so-li nel giar-din.

Ars. Te-mer non vo-glio fin-chè il tuo A-mor, o mia ger-ma-na, è in so-glio. *(parte)*

Scena ii
Rosana e Gerina

84. *Recitativo*

Rosana: Eh, se in-cau-ta tu sei, stol-ta non so-no. Non si per-dan di vi-sta l'or-me del re, del-lo stra-nier, sin tan-to che non piom-ba sul reo la mia ven-det-ta. Si e-splo-ri o-gni pen-sie-ro ed o-gni ac-cen-to, tem-po non gli si do-ni di sve-la-re il mio er-ror; chi pri-mo ac-cu-sa, se in-no-cen-te non è lo sem-bra al-me-no.

143

85. Aria

144

Dio d'a-mor, ca - - - - - - - - - - de, ca-de e-

stin-to il Dio d'a-mor, e-stin-to il Dio d'a-mor.

E da que - sta so-lo a-spet-ta qual-che pa - - - ce il me - sto cor,

e da que-sta so-lo a-spet-ta qual-che pa - - ce il me-sto cor, il me - sto, il me-sto cor.

Da capo

145

86. Recitativo

(Rosana si ritira)
Gerina

O quan - to, o quan-to sa ques-ta pa-dro - na mia! E' scal - tra, è fi - ne, è

le - sta; ma fra tut - te le don - ne ad es-ser ta - le non è so - la ques-ta. Ho un gran ti -

mo - re del mio ca-ro Er-sin-do, chè la don-na ta-lor s'è dis-prez - za - ta è peg-gio d'u-na fu-ria sca-te-na-ta.

87. *Aria*

Spiritoso

Violino I

Violino II

Viola

Gerina

Continuo

In sen mi pal - - - - pi-ta tre-man - te il cor, e per quel

O Dio! non fos - se mai, mai qui ve - nu - to o non l'a - ves - si mai co - no - sciu - to, mai co - no -

sciu - to chè non a - vrei sì rio mar - tir; non fos - se mai, mai qui ve - nu - to e non l'a - ves - si mai co - no - sciu - to che non a -

vrei sì rio mar - tir_____, sì rio mar - tir_____, non a - vrei sì rio_____, sì rio_____ mar - tir.

Da capo

88. *Recitativo accompagnato*

Di Flo-ra al-le lu-sin-ghe o-ve so-ven-te scen-do del re-gno a se-re-nar le cu-re, l'ar-mo-nia di tue

vo-ci ag-giun-gi, Er-sin-do. Ve-gli, ve-gli in-fin, ch'io ri-po-so sui miei son-ni il tuo can-to al piè del tro-no,

Adagio

chè i ri-po-si dei Gran-di o-zio non so-no.

Mustafa

(O___ ___che buo-na for-tu-na! Io vo-glio sta-re in-tan-to qui-vi a-sco-so a sen-tir d'Er-sin-do il can-to.)

89. Aria

90. Recitativo

Così una fida amante scherzar soleva in armonia di pene del l'avvinto suo ben sulle catene; con latte di speranza o temprava il suo duolo o in vita mantenea la sua costanza. Già stendea l'infelice la destra almeno a sollevarle i ceppi quando, ahi caso fatal! Donna tiranna per un mal nato amore ambi divise, e la speranza, nata appena, uccise.

91. *Recitativo*

92. *Aria*

Er - sin - do fa co - rag - gio, fa co - rag - gio, deh la - scia, la - scia, la - scia il te -

mer; Er - sin - do fa co - rag - gio, deh la - scia, la - scia,

la - scia di te-mer, deh la - - - - - - -

scia,   la - scia di te - mer.   Ri -

mi - ra___ la ro - sa   ch'è tin - ta di san - gue per far - si più gra - ta al no - stro pia-cer;   ri - mi - ra la ro - sa ch'è

tin - ta di san - gue per far - si più gra - ta al no - stro pia-cer_____,   al no - stro pia - cer.

Da capo

154

Mustafà, Ridolfo condotto dai soldati
con le mani legate da dietro, e detti

93. *Recitativo*

* See Introduction.

Rosana esce con Arsace, Gerina e detti

94. Recitativo

95. Quartetto

muor lo sprez - za - tor_____, lo sprez-za - tor, sprez-za - tor, sprez-za - tor. Reo mi fe - sti, reo,

reo mi fe - sti, e ti per - do - no, ti per - do - no, ti per-do - no. Del tuo dan - no la di-

scol - pa, O in-fe - li - ce, in-fe - li - ce è mio do-lor_____, è mio do-lor, è mio do-

Reo mi fe - sti,

Cunegonda e Ridolfo

96. Duetto

Ernesto condotto dalle guardie e detti

97. *Recitativo*

....Ri - dol - fo, ad - dio. Se tu ri - ma - ni in vi - ta, in pe - gno del mio a -

mor pren - di il mio re - gno, e al - la pa - tria rap - por - ta che per sal - var - ti Cu - ne - gon - da è mor - ta.

98. *Aria*

Andante lento

Ri - cor - da-ti, ri -

cor - da-ti di me mia vi - ta, mia vi - ta, mia vi - ta ad - di - o;

ri - cor - da-ti di me, di me, di me ri - cor - da-ti, mia vi - ta ad-dio mia

vi - ta ad-di - o, mia vi - ta ad-dio, ad-dio mia vi - ta ad-di - o, ad - dio, ad-dio.

La fè che ti do-nai co - stan - te ti ser-bai si - no a mo-rir per te, i - do-lo mi - o, si -

no a mo-rir per te, i - do-lo mi - o, mo - rir, mo-rir per te, i - do-lo mi - o.

Da capo

162

99. *Recitativo*

100. *Aria*

....Per ri-con-dur-re al tro-no il suo a-ma-to Ri-dol-fo, il Pren-ce di Ger-ma-nia è quel-lo, e quel-lo io so-no.

Gri - de - rà stra-ge e ven-det - - ta il mio san - gue

tin - to d'i - ra e di fu - ror_____, e di fu - ror;

stra - ge e ven-det-ta, ven-det-ta, ven-det - - ta gri-de-rà il mio san - gue

tin - to d'i - - ra e di fu - ror, gri-de-rà____

, tin - to d'i - ra e di fu - ror____

164

101. *Recitativo*

Si, gri - de - ran ven - det - ta al Cie - lo pu - ni - tor l'om - bre tra - di - te; ma per - chè ti - ran - nia gli Dei non

te - me, di quel - la al - men pa - ven - ti, che un gior - no por - te - ran con spa - de ul - tri - ci so - pra l'A - fri - ca tut - ta i re - gni a - mi - ci.

102. *Aria*

Con - tro l'E - git - to, con - tro l'E - git - to Cie - lo e

ter - ra s'ar - me - rà, con - tro l'E - git - to Cie - lo e ter - ra, Cie - lo e ter - ra s'ar - me -

103. *Recitativo*

Miei fi - di, en - tro il più chiu - so del par - co o-gnun di lor sia cu - sto - di - to.

A - vran - no tut - ti in - os - ser - va - ta mor - te; ma, che fa - vel - li Ar - sa - ce?

Pen - sa pria che con es - si di Ro - sa - na l'er - ror non può mo - ri - re. So - lo dei rei la

fu - ga as - si - cu - rar - ci può. Co - sì, co - sì ri - sol - vo. O - là! Si - gnor, che im -

po - ni? Gui - da que-gli schia-vi al por - to, o - ve di lie - te fa - ci nel-la not-te vi-ci - na per le vit-to - rie

mie splen - don le na - vi. I - vi dei miei guer - rie - ri a - be - te ar - ma - to gli ser - vi - rà di

scor - ta ai lo - ro pi - ni, ed i - vi m'at-ten - di. (O me fe - li - ce!) E - se - gui-rò i tuoi cen - ni.

(Con lo - ro io vo - glio an - da - re, e Ge - ri - na e l'a-mor pos - son cre - pa - re.)

168

104. *Aria*

169

lo, ru-bel-lo ed è fe - del, ed è fe - del_____, ed è fe-

del.

E' giu - sto, è giu-sto a-ver ti-

mo — re di ti -ran-nia_____, di ti-ran-nia cru-del,

giu-sto a-ver ti-mo — re di ti-ran-nia, di ti-ran-nia cru-del_____, di ti-ran-nia cru-del.

Da capo

170

Scena xii

Camera
Gerina e poi Mustafà in abito da donna

105. *Recitativo*

Eppur la gran paz-zi-a, la gran paz-zi-a il di-sprez-zar l'a-mo-re! Quel mi-se-ro d'Er-sin-do, ne ho pur la gran pas-sio-ne, dev' es-ser sa-et-ta-to per a-ver di-sprez-za-to l'a-mor del-la pa-dro-na. Or io non son co-sì du-ra di co-re, chè ta-lor se ri-mi-ro un che mi por-ta af-fet-to se po-tes-si, il por-rei den-tro il mio pet-to.

106. *Aria*

Io con tut-ti scher-zo e ri-do, scher-zo, ri-do, nè so far mai la ri-tro-sa mai, mai, nè so

Dal segno al ⁀ e poi il ritornello

Ritornello

172

107. *Recitativo*

173

sti-to. Nol pos-so dir. Ma pu-re? Al-tri tem-pi, al-tre cu-re. Ah, in-gan-na-to-re! (Io vo' sco-pri-re al-fin.) Cer-to che

que-sto stra-ta-gem-ma è d'a-mor. (Che a-scol-to mai? Chi sen-te ge-lo-sia fe-ri-to ha il co-re.) Ah, i-ni-quo, ah, in-

gra-to! E' que-sta, è que-sta la fè che m'hai pro-mes-sa? (Io non m'in-gan-no al cer-to: il pro-ver-bo non fal-la, che l'a-mo-re giam-

mai può star co-per-to.) Non do-ve-vi pia-gar-mi se vo-le-vi la-sciar-mi. (Che fo? Gliel di-co? Non tra-dir-mi A-

mo-re.) Cru-del, cru-del. Sen-ti mio co-re, ma pro-met-ti si-len-zio. Io lo pro-met-to.

(♭)

Per-chè da te sprez-za-to a-ve-vo ri-so-lu-to di fug-gir-me-ne or or con cer-ti schia-vi.

(Che sen-to?) E chi son que-sti? Ri-dol-fo, Er-sin-do e Er-ne-sto, e tu sa-rai mia spo-sa ed

io tuo spo-so. Io son con-ten-ta, e quan-do an-diam, mio be-ne? Or o-ra. Oh che gran gio-ia! E do-ve ti ri-tro-vo, i-do-lo

mio? Al gran por-ton t'a-spet-to. Ver-rai, ver-rai, mio bel tre-sor? Sì, sì, mio di-let-to.

174

108. *Duetto*

Di ve-der-ti già mi

pa - re del-l'Eu-ro-pa al bel pae-se con le ve-sti al-la fran-ce - se   far___ pro-fon-de ri - ve-ren - ze, ri-ve-ren-ze quan-do ve - di

Di ve-der-ti an-che a me pa-re gir ga-lan-te per la stra-da col ba-ston, cap-pel-lo e spa-da   a me

il tuo mon-siù,   mon-siù,   mon-siù.

far più ri-ve-ren - ze, ri-ve-ren - ze ed io dir - ti   ad - dio mon - siù,   mon - siù,   mon-siù.

Vie-ni,

Dal segno

177

Aladino e Rosanà

109. *Recitativo*

110. *Aria*

111. *Recitativo*

Gerina: Uh si-gno-ra, si-gno-ra...

Rosana: Che re-chi?

Ger.: O se sa-pes-si che tra-di-men-to c'è!

Aladino: Che tra-di-men-to?

(6)

Ger.: Mu-sta-fà tra-ve-sti-to sen fug-ge con Er-sin-do e gli al-tri schia-vi.

Ros.: Che sen-to!

Alad.: E co-me? E

Ger.: quan-do? O-ra, e al por-to m'a-spet-ta, chè per sco-prir l'ar-ca-no pro-mi-si anch' io fug-gir.

Alad.: O Ar-sa-ce in-de-gno!

Ros.: Mio

(6)

Alad.: re? Ros.: Ta-ci. (Pa-ven-to del ger-ma-no.) Alad.: A miei pie-di ca-drà quel ca-po in-de-gno che non sep-pe e-se-gui-re un

mio co-man-do. Ros.: Ah, Ge-ri-na! Il ger-ma-no sta in ri-schio. Ger.: Io che sa-pea di Ar-sa-ce?

Ma che im-por-ta? Con le lu-sin-ghe vo-stre ben po-tre-te fre-nar l'i-ra al re-gnan-te. Ros.: A-mor m'as-

si-sta in tal pe-ri-glio e-stre-mo e scoc-chi i stra-li suoi dal mio sem-bian-te.

112. *Aria*

Con mil - le e mil - le vez - - zi si pla-chi e s'ac-ca-rez -
zi l'i-ra-to re-gna-tor, l'i-ra - to, l'i-ra - to re-gna-tor;

con mil-le e mil-le vez - - zi si pla-ca e s'ac-ca - rez - zi l'i - ra - - -

- - - to, l'i - ra - to re-gna-tor, l'i-ra - - - - - - to, l'i-

ra - to re-gna-tor.

Se ac-qui-sta pre-mio e lo - de un' in-ge-gno-sa fro - de che ser - ve a un gran - de a-

mor, se ac-qui-sta pre-mio e lo - de un' in-ge-gno - sa fro - de che ser - ve a un gran - de a-mor_____, un

gran - - - - - - - - - de, un gran - de a-mor.

Dal segno

Porto con nave alla riva illuminata,
con altre navi anche illuminate in
tempo di notte, con luna in cielo
Cunegonda, Ridolfo, Arsace, Ernesto e Mustafà

113. *Recitativo*

Sia-mo sal-vi, Ri-dol-fo? Sì, mio be-ne. Tut-ti sal-vi già sie-te,

e ac-ciò più cer-ta sia la vo-stra sa-lu-te io ne ven-go a scor-tar la vo-stra fu-ga.

114. *Duetto*

Or che ren-di a que-sto pie-de la sua ca-ra, ca-ra, ca-ra li-ber-tà,

giu-sto pre-mio la mia fe-de ti pro-met-te e ti da-rà;

giu - sto, giu - sto pre - mio la mia fe - de ti pro-met - te e ti da - rà_____

_____, e ti da - rà.

Cunegonda

Or che il be - ne tu mi ren - di che sol bra - ma, che sol

bra - ma que - sto cor, quel - la glo - ria tu con - ten - di ch'è de - sio_____ del

Dio d'a - mor; quel - la glo - ria tu con - ten - di ch'è de -

sio____, de-sio del Dio d'a-mor_____

_____, de-sio del Dio d'a-mor.

#6   6   #

115. *Recitativo*

Ridolfo

Arsace

Ar - sa - ce, ad-dio.   Lun - gi n'an-drem. Fer - ma - te.   Pria di par-tir io vo - glio

Continuo

pe-gno di vo-stra fè, che giun-ti al re-gno mai non si ten-te-rà dal-le vo-str'ar-mi guer-ra con-tro l'E-git-to.

Rid.

Sa Ri-dol-fo es-ser gra-to an-che ai ne-mi-ci. Tan-to pro-met-to e in pe-gno di mia fe-de e di

#4

Ars.

quel-la del-la mia Cu-ne-gon-da ec-co la de-stra. Co-sì al re ser-vo ed a me stes-so an-co-ra.

6

186

Aladino, Rosana, Gerina, guardie con faci e detti

116. *Recitativo*

cor. (Ro-sa-na, io tac-cio l'ac-cu-sa tua.) (Per-do-na, o prin-ci-pes-sa, u-na col-pa che fu col-pa d'a-

Rid.

mo-re.) Ah! Bra-mar più non sa con-ten-to il co-re. Me pre-sen-te con-giun-ga A-mor le vo-stre pal-me, e tu Ro-sa-na

Alad.

Ros.

O con-ten-ti! Con-giun-ga le no-stre al-me il Nu-me In-fan-te.

Rid.

O pia-ce-ri! Con-giun-ga le no-stre al-me il Nu-me In-fan-te.

Cun.

O pia-ce-ri! Con-giun-ga le no-stre al-me il Nu-me In-fan-te.

(Alad.)

sten-di la de-stra a me, spo-sa e re-gnan-te. O con-ten-ti! Con-giun-ga le no-stre al-me il Nu-me In-fan-te.

(Alad.)

Già, che be-ni-gno il cie-lo de-gno mi fe di sì gran sor-te: a-mi-ci, non vi fia gra-ve

Rid.

l'o-no-rar le mie noz-ze col vo-stro a-spet-to, e al vo-stro ciel na-tio vi sa-rò scor-ta io stes-so. A un sì gran re nul-la ne-

Cun.

Mus.

gar si puo-te. Mia bel-la, ec-co-ci in cal-ma. Giu-bi-la in sen per il pia-cer quest' al-ma. Già ch'è dì d'al-le-grez-za, si-

Alad.

Ger.

Ros.

gnor, deh ti con-ten-ta ch'io mi spo-si a Ge-ri-na. Io son pa-go. Ma pria dee con-ten-tar-si la pa-dro-na mi-a. An-cor io son con-

(Ros.)

Ger.

ten-ta. Ec-co la man. Mio so-le, a me piac-cio-no i fat-ti, e non pa-ro-le.

Mus.

Dam-mi la man. Mio so-le, a me piac-cio-no i fat-ti, e non pa-ro-le.

188

117. *Ensemble*

189

Fine dell'Opera

LIBRETTO

Cast of Characters

Aladino, Sultan of Egypt
Rosana, his reigning favorite
Ridolfo, Prince of Germany and a captive in Egypt
Cunegonda, Princess of Bohemia, betrothed to Ridolfo, in the garb of a man, under
    the name of Ersindo
Arsace, military general of the sultan, and Rosana's brother
Ernesto, admiral of Cunegonda's fleet, and Ridolfo's confidant
Gerina, Rosana's lady-in-waiting
Mustafà, guardian of the captives

There are numerous short passages of recitative in the printed libretto of 1710 which are "virgolated" (marked with a double comma ,, at the beginning of each line) and for which Scarlatti wrote no music. These virgolated lines are omitted in the present translation. However, those portions of Acts I and III which are lacking in the present edition because of missing folios in the manuscript sources (see Introduction) have been retained in the translation and are indicated by brackets in the margin.

ACT I

Scene i

Shore at the mouth of the Nile, with a hut on one side, from which CUNEGONDA *and* ERNESTO *come forth. A little boat, which has furnished their transport, and which will serve Ernesto to go in search of the fleet scattered by the storm.*

CUN. I was the plaything of the storm, but my kind star will at last have pity on me, nor shall I be glad or happy if it does not make peace with me and give me my beloved. Let us go.

ERN. No, princess. Let Ernesto go.

CUN. And shall I remain here alone on the shore, the prey of sorrow?

ERN. In that hut, and guarded by the kind shepherd who saved us from the sea, you will have more peace and less danger.

CUN. Ernesto, I prefer death to seeing myself here alone and abandoned.

ERN. Grant a delay on which both freedom and well-being depend.

CUN. Go then, but know that you take with you, O faithful man, all my hopes.

ERN. And with you remain mine, those of the kingdom, and of the bridegroom himself.
Do not despair, no, no, for Heaven will show itself piteous toward you, and, even if it was harsh to you earlier, it will at last give you a happy repose. (*Enters the boat and departs.*)

Scene ii
CUNEGONDA

CUN. You have departed, O Ernesto, and I remain weeping, for, if the sea did not take pity on my misfortunes, Egypt, with Ridolfo a captive and Cunegonda bled white, will do so. But to make my heart happy, interrupt my sorrow for a moment, O my eyes, with the charming portrait of my beloved. (*Takes out Ridolfo's picture and looks at it.*) Beloved Ridolfo, behold, to follow the light of your fair eyes, faithful Cunegonda despises all cruel outrages of evil fate.

Scene iii

Arsace, military general of the sultan, cast ashore by the storm, disembarks with his troops to take water.
CUNEGONDA, *later* ARSACE.

CUN. What, Egyptian soldiers here! Ah, I am lost! What shall I do? Let me flee!

ARS. Some of your soldiers follow him; that foreign garb, and flight on the arrival of our arms, makes him either an enemy of Egypt or a criminal. Meanwhile, my warriors, cool your burning lips in the outlet of the Nile. (CUNEGONDA *is brought in, captured by the soldiers.*) Young man, to whom nature gave such a noble face, why did you run away from our armed strength?

CUN. It is no wonder if a stranger flees from the sight of armed men.

ARS. A stranger? and why alone?

CUN. I am a humble survivor of the shipwreck that has overtaken my many companions; my name is Ersindo, Germany is my homeland; there is the whole story of my adventures told in a single breath.

ARS. Add further to these, that you are my captive.

CUN. Eternal gods! And this, this is the last and greatest of my woes.

ARS. Do not complain, for perhaps your fate is less cruel than you fear.

CUN. Is it perhaps a slight misfortune, barely to escape the arms of death, only to meet with chains?

ARS. Listen: indeed it is an unchangeable law that he who is the captive of our arms must stretch out his foot for the gyves of servitude. You, nevertheless, will come to the court of Egypt as a companion rather than as a prisoner. Escort him, soldiers, to my ships. Come, young man, for your countenance will be greatly softened by your fate.
Often, Heaven seems hostile and then, appeased, 7 does not shoot its arrows; but sometimes, when it seems peaceful, it then more vigorously shows forth its vengefulness.

Scene iv
CUNEGONDA

CUN. Let us go happily, for perhaps Fate will appear 8 one day, appeased, in the shape of Ridolfo.
I come, Love, where I am called by some flash of 9 brightness from my fate. Even death is made palatable by a single glance from my beloved. (*Exit, followed by soldiers.*)

Scene v

Rosana's room. GERINA *and pages.*

GER. Quick, quick, boys, bring the table, for your 10 mistress wishes to make herself beautiful. She is so beautiful and kind that I can say no evil of her; nor do I do like so-and-so does, who does not refrain from telling to this one and that, for every trifle, things about her mistress which perhaps she ought to keep secret. (*Pages bring table.*)
There are certain damsels who, acting modest and 11 saddish, go around saying: "My mistress makes love with so-and-so, and gives him her soul and her heart, and writes to him, in letters of gold: For you I am tormented, for you I die"; I, however, do not act that way. I only say that mine, if she behaves crossly, she does it only to give pleasure to her husband, whom she is to have, and thinks of him night and day.
But it is time to call her. Oh, this is a fine mess! 12 Where is the mirror, where is the casket, the aloes and the perfume? If she gets angry, she will make you weep this morning. What an accursed race are pages! (*Pages bring in the chair which* ROSANA *is to sit in to be made beautiful.*) Quick, quick, like this; put it on top of here. Eh! They are never good for anything, if one does not use the whip on them. But here comes my mistress right now.

Scene vi
ROSANA *and* GERINA

ROS. Thanks, since my sovereign lover is already 13 pleased with you through my countenance. Strengthen the enchantments by which you make his heart the prisoner of my beauty.

GER. O revered madam, come, for all is now ready here.

ROS. I entrust myself to you; and you, my faithful one, set my hair in the most attractive waywardness which can make my appearance the most charming.

GER. Leave it to me; you know full well that I have a delicate taste; I shall bedeck you with ribbons and flowers in such a way that the sultan will adore you today. (ROSANA *sings the aria while beautifying herself at the table.*)

14 ROS. A mannerism, a glance from a fair face is never slow in making a man fall in love. Whether he adores, or pretends to, in a moment with flattery I know how to enchain him.

15 GER. Madam, if you permit, this curl is out of place; and then, if you are willing, I wish to add a beauty-spot on this cheek, which will make your whiteness seem brighter to the gallant sultan, wherefore he will die of love for you.

Scene vii
ROSANA, GERINA, *and* MUSTAFÀ

16 MUS. With my usual confidence I come, madam, to pay you homage.

ROS. What news do you bring?

MUS. The great sultan is coming here to pay homage to you.

GER. Hurry, hurry! Quickly, quickly hide everything. (*The pages carry away the table and chair.*)

MUS. Gerina?

GER. I'm busy now. Can't you see? Use a little bit of sense.

MUS. Here is the sultan.

GER. Now, charms and flattery, get to work.

Scene viii
ROSANA, GERINA, MUSTAFÀ, *and* ALADINO

17 ALA. My belovéd?

ROS. You here, my king, my god?

ALA. I return to the brilliance of your rays, my fair lady.

ROS. Nay, rather, it is you, my sun, who bring them to my countenance.

GER. (What honeyed words!)

ALA. It is enough, my beloved; wait a short while for love to be the center of attention.

ROS. My soul will be in torment.

ALA. Arsace comes today, as a victor, into my royal presence.

ROS. Arsace a victor! O happy news!

ALA. (*To* MUSTAFÀ) Have Arsace enter immediately.

MUS. I hasten to inform him.

Scene ix
ROSANA, GERINA, MUSTAFÀ, ALADINO, *and* ARSACE

18 ROS. (Now that my brother receives the palms, let us advance more boldly to the throne.)

MUS. Here he is, my lord.

ARS. I bring to your kingly feet, Sire, your victories rather than mine. On hearing, even from afar, the noise of your arms, the Arabs and the Persians were already vanquished; and Heaven gave victory and peace to Arsace as reward for his faithfulness.

ROS. (And what foreign youth, with a thousand graces in his countenance, is he bringing with him?)

GER. (O how attractive he is! I like him very much.)

ALA. General, see the pleasure of your return welcomed on my countenance.

MUS. (See that she-devil, on beholding that stranger, how fixedly she stares at him!)

ROS. My lord, Arsace and I vie in kissing the shining footsteps of your royal favor.

ARS. In addition to the palms of victory, O Sire, we must give you a conquest made just now in Egypt.

ALA. What might it be?

ARS. This young man, who has outstanding ability in singing and in playing; he has shown himself fit to be a worthy gift.

ALA. He is very pleasing to me, Arsace, both because of the hand which gives him, and because of his appearance; but most for his skill, in which I delight.

GER. (He surely is good-looking!)

MUS. (Oh, how jealousy gnaws at my bosom!)

ROS. Of what name, what rank, and what country is he? (Certainly not all of Africa ever contained such beauty.)

ARS. You shall learn about him. Young man, speak.

CUN. My name is Ersindo. I am, though unfortunate, of noble birth in Germany, for my unlucky star robbed me at a fated moment of my country and my good fortune.

ROS. (What sweet speech!)

GER. (I feel pity for him.)

MUS. (And does she keep her gaze fixed on him? Now I can't stand it any longer.) (MUSTAFÀ *passes over to the other side to where* GERINA *is.*)

ARS. And what fate brought you to these shores?

CUN. I was moved by the fame of such a great king and such a vast empire.

MUS. (*Sotto voce to* GERINA) Won't you lower your eyes?

GER. What harm is there in looking at a stranger?

ALA. Did you come alone?

CUN. Alone, because, of those who came with me, I was the only one to survive the storm; but this is not the greatest of my woes.

ALA. But you are safe in Egypt, and pleasing to the king; what have you to complain of?

CUN. Of cruel captivity.

ALA. You have no chains.

CUN. (I am complaining of another's chains, not my own.)

ARS. In fact, from the moment when he became my captive, I gave him freedom.

ALA. I confirm it for him.

ROS. (He who is born to captivate others, is no captive himself.)

ALA. Rosana, I appoint him to the honor of your court.

ROS. (O happy me!) He will have, among my dearest people (and in my heart) a rank suitable to his deserts (and to his fair countenance).

ALA. Farewell, Rosana. I await your fair presence to render agreeable the horror of the coming battle.

ROS. I am ready, Sire, and Ersindo will be with me.

ALA. Follow me, Arsace, and let your arrival reflect glory upon the pomp of the customary show.

MUS. I hasten to choose the captives. Use your brains, Gerina. Get me?

GER. I get you, yes.

MUS. Good-bye, my dear. (*Exit.*)

CUN. (Ah, if I do not see my Ridolfo, this show will be only sorrowful for me.)

19 ALA. In the arena, where horror dwells, let there be play, and let the god of love smile there. In the light of your countenance let the mortal blade become fairer, which is the object of horror.

Scene x
ROSANA, CUNEGONDA, *and* GERINA

20 ROS. My heart, let us discover the character of the recently arrived stranger

GER. (It seems to me that my mistress is already melting in the light of those eyes.)

ROS. Ersindo, do you still complain of the misadventures you have endured?

CUN. For an unhappy person, one moment of well-being does not change his feelings.

ROS. Received by the sovereign and caressed (and, I almost said, loved by Rosana), can you fear any misfortunes?

CUN. The favors of a king do not succeed in curing the misfortunes of the heart.

GER. (I am sorry for his misfortunes.)

ROS. Are you perhaps in love?

CUN. You have spoken rightly.

ROS. With a fortunate love?

CUN. On the contrary, unhappy.

ROS. (Let us hope that Love finds a place in that bosom.) Where is the object of your love?

CUN. In Egypt.

ROS. (Were I that person!) How is it that your love is in Egypt, if you came here by yourself?

CUN. He has been breathing the air of these skies for a long time.

ROS. Can I be of aid to you?

CUN. Without greater risk, you cannot, and, if you could, you would not want to.

GER. (Too veiled a speech!)

ROS. Is he of Africa, or of Europe?

CUN. Ah, my queen, ask no more.

ROS. I wish to do your pleasure. Confide more fully in me, Ersindo; say in what way I can help you, for if I can, I shall be willing to do so. Do not make your misfortune harder by your silence.

21 You are silent, and do not know that he who keeps his love silent suffers double torment. Speak, and you will see that, by telling your sorrows, your lips will become the salvation of your heart. (*Exit.*)

22 GER. Fair youth, if you wish to be happy, speak, do not remain silent; and, to prove this true, listen to a saying of my teacher: if you keep your mouth shut, you'll never get any soup in it.

Scene xi
CUNEGONDA

23 CUN. Let us go in search of Ridolfo, O my emotions, for my misfortunes will point him out to you. If an unhappy wretch is moved towards you as much as, or more than, myself, that man is Ridolfo—that Ridolfo who, although he was chosen for a royal match from among many great and fortunate friends, must now be sought among the unfortunate.

24 I sigh for you, I seek you, I call you, and in my bosom you are my life, my treasure, but such as I desire you I would wish to have you in my heart and in my bosom.

Scene xii
Amphitheater for the slaughter of the captives by the Mamelukes; an elevated place for the court. MUSTAFÀ, *and later* RIDOLFO *with the other captives.*

25 MUS. The fighting between the captives and the Mamelukes will make a pretty sight today! The one advances and attacks the other, the other defends himself bravely; the one moves forward, the other replies, the one opposes and is confounded and falls to the ground. Those captives who have a base heart have as their punishment a cruel death, and those others who have bravery receive freedom as their reward.

26 But it must be time now to open the doors for those captives. (*Enter* RIDOLFO *with the other captives, and the Mamelukes.*) Come on, come, and behave like brave men, for it is no question of trifles here; and if you have good sense, do your best to keep your skin intact. You, Mamelukes, go over there, and know how to use skill against skill.

RID. Companions, now is the moment in which fate decides for us, either liberty or death. A happy death I would call it, if I could remove from my thoughts both Cunegonda and worry about her faithfulness. What worry! After two years, with no news even of her sorrow, doubt lest I have been betrayed is already certitude. Yes, she believes me dead, or wishes me so. Cruel one, you will be satisfied, here I am facing death; but expect a lofty vengeance on your couch and on your throne.

27 Say, for it is my shade betrayed, whether you hear your rest disturbed. Say, for it is the blood of your betrothed, whether you feel a blush on your face. That remorse which does not come from the thought of my fetters, when I have left this life I hope to cause you from the Elysian Fields.

Scene xiii
MUSTAFÀ, RIDOLFO *with the other captives, and* ARSACE

28 ARS. Base herd of captives, this is the day to gain a better standing for your fate, through bravery.

RID. General, since fate chooses today for me to end my sorrows, I ask a favor of you, which it is a sin to deny to the unhappy.

ARS. What might it be?

RID. That I be granted the fatal advantage of being the first to enter the lists.

MUS. (That fellow must be brave!)

ARS. Your thought is as desperate as your wish is unfair. I may not decide what is placed in Fortune's keeping. Wait, on one side, for the customary sign which challenges you to combat, for the sight of the sultan changes the horror of fate into delight.

29 War, slaughter, blood, and death are the boast of the king's pleasure. These make the sovereign stronger

and make the vassal bolder and more warlike.

30   MUS. (*To* RIDOLFO) Do what I tell you, buddy. Don't expose yourself to so much risk, for losing your life is a big mess.

  RID. Let us go, companions, for death is a good thing when it comes to extricate us finally from troubles.

31   I gladly face the sight of death; I have a heart of adamant which has no fear. In the doom of an unyielding fate this heart will know how to resist unflinchingly. (*Exit with other captives.*)

Scene xiv
ALADINO, ROSANA, CUNEGODA, ARSACE, *and* MUSTAFÀ

ARS. Sire, everything is ready.

ALA. I rely on you; follow me. (*Goes and sits with* ROSANA.)

CUN. (But where are the captives, where is my beloved?)

ARS. Let the trumpet give the customary signal. (*Here a soldier brings to the sultan's feet the urn with the names of the captives who are to fight.*) My lord, whom does the king's sign designate to draw the first fighter from the urn?

ALA. The young man from Europe.

32   CUN. (Unhappy honor!)

ARS. Here are the names of the captives. Go near the king, and give me the name of the first of the poor wretches.

CUN. (And shall I be able to stretch out my right hand to the urn, in which is perhaps the fate of my Ridolfo?)

ARS. Young man, make haste.

CUN. (Delay is of no use; my hand trembles at the risk.) Here it is. (Ah, what anguish!) (CUNEGONDA *extracts a name and* ARSACE *reads*)

ARS. Aristarchus of Greece.

CUN. (O Heaven! I breathe again.)

MUS. Now we shall see who wins. (*The combat follows, with unequal weapons, and with the death of the captive.*) Oh, poor chap!

CUN. (Is the combat so unequal?)

ARS. Let the second be drawn.

CUN. (And danger presses even more strongly. Help me, O Love!) (CUNEGONDA *draws another name, and* ARSACE *reads*)

ARS. Sigismondo of Italy.

CUN. (My wish has been fulfilled for a second time.) (*The second combat takes place, ending like the first with the death of the captive.*)

MUS. He, too, has fallen.

ARS. Keep on, young man.

CUN. (And is barbarism not yet fully sated with two deaths? Let us continue and see who it is; but if it is Ridolfo?) (CUNEGONDA *extracts the third name, and* ARSACE *reads*)

ARS. Ridolfo of Germany.

Scene xv
ALADINO, ROSANA, CUNEGONDA, ARSACE, *and* MUSTAFA. *Enter* RIDOLFO *to fight; later,* GERINA

CUN. (Ah, ill-fated name!) (CUNEGONDA *draws forth the picture of Ridolfo, and scans it*). (It is he, I see him already and recognize him; but recognizing him, O ye Gods, costs me too dearly!)

RID. At last my death draws near. Cunegonda, here is the fatal blow, and perhaps yet, if it does not come from your hand, it comes from your heart.

CUN. (And does he die with my name on his lips?)

RID. Young man, if a pitiless lady ever chances one day to inquire after Ridolfo, tell her that, to fulfill a cruel wish of hers, Ridolfo has died.

CUN. (My heart is breaking, nor can I say "My prince!")

ALA. Ho there! Is the fierce battle still delayed?

CUN. (There is after all no escape.)

RID. Let us go to meet death. (RIDOLFO *begins the combat.*)

CUN. My lord, Rosana, Arsace, I am fainting. (*At this point* CUNEGONDA *faints at Rosana's feet. The court arise at the unexpected event, and the combat is broken off.*)

ROS. What is the matter, Ersindo?

ALA. What is the matter? (ARSACE *holds up* CUNEGONDA, *who has fainted.*)

ARS. I am holding him.

GER. I have arrived on time. Ooh, poor chap! With this liquor, which is very strong, he may revive.   33

RID. (What delay is interfering with my rest?)

ROS. Death, which is hovering over this arena, is coming to Ersindo's cheeks.

ALA. Weak young man! Let the combat be immediately stopped for the present, and put off until another day. What news, Arsace?

ARS. He is returning to his senses.

GER. He has already regained his cheer.

ROS. (At last I breathe again!)

CUN. Who is calling me back to life?

ROS. Rosana (who adores you).

ALA. The king, who is fond of you.

ARS. Go, wretches; your fate is postponed until the dawn of another day.

RID. Ah, how slow death is when an unhappy man yearns for it. (*Exit.*)

MUS. You there, take out those corpses quickly, and then go back in again, for there will be no more fighting today. (*The captives remove the corpses, and* MUSTAFA *shuts them in again.*)

Scene xvi
CUNEGONDA, ALADINO, ROSANA, ARSACE, *and* GERINA

CUN. (Is Ridolfo safe? Let every sorrow vanish.)   34

ALA. Ersindo, why this distress?

CUN. (What shall I say?) My lord, I have such a soft heart that just one drop of blood is enough to sicken it.

GER. (It is just about like mine.)

ARS. Such a cowardly spirit is unworthy, Ersindo, of such a fair countenance.

ALA. I wish you to be firmer at later encounters.

CUN. My glance will have to become accustomed and resist a stronger attack, another day. (But if Ridolfo is endangered, I shall return to my former distress.)

ALA. Your heart is too timorous, now that you return to freedom. If I strike the gyves from your feet, you can still hope for mercy from a love which is on the throne. (*Exit with* ARSACE.)   35

Scene xvii
ROSANA, CUNEGONDA, GERINA, *and later* MUSTAFÀ

36 ROS. Your distress, Ersindo, has another cause than the horror you conceived.

CUN. You have guessed it.

ROS. And where does it come from?

CUN. From love.

GER. (I knew it already; my heart told me so.)

ROS. Does love torment your heart so cruelly that it brings you to the point of fainting with sorrow?

CUN. The sight of my beloved (and what a cruel sight!) caused my trouble

ROS. Did you see her, and was she present at the show?

CUN. My beloved had a great part in it.

ROS. (I saw no other woman.)

GER. (When he fainted, I had not yet arrived.)

ROS. Did you speak to her?

CUN. Ah, I had to remain silent, and my silence was my executioner.

ROS. (It is worthwhile to go further.) Was she near, or far from you?

CUN. (I have gone too far.)

ROS. Come on, speak!

CUN. Ah, you tempt me any more in vain; if I did not say it for fear of death, I shall all the less say it to satisfy your wish.

ROS. But would there be anyone to whom you might tell it, at least?

CUN. There would be, and not far away.

GER. (Oh, I wish I were she.)

ROS. (It seems that he is always talking for me.) Now make him known to me.

CUN. A European captive, who has the same fatherland as I, and whom I saw exposed to the great hazard together with the other captives.

ROS. And would you reveal your love to him?

CUN. With great pleasure.

ROS: I shall console you (and satisfy myself at the same time). Let Mustafà come hither!

CUN. Here he comes.

ROS. Take Ersindo to the prison, and have a certain captive, with whom he wishes to speak, come forth under escort.

MUS. I shall obey (*To* CUNEGONDA) Your lordship may go towards the prison, and I shall come immediately also. (Now my beloved keeps me here.)

CUN. (I shall finally be allowed to look upon my beloved without risk.) I obey a command which agrees with my desires and my feelings.

37 When you shall see the arrow which I have in my bosom, you will have pity on it, for to uncover a mortal wound and not to heal it, is cruelty. (*Exit.*)

Scene xviii
ROSANA, GERINA, *and* MUSTAFÀ

38 GER. Go!

MUS. Where?

GER. With Ersindo.

MUS. Now I have something to do. I have told him where he is to wait for me.

ROS. Hope and fear, which of you shall I trust? He flatters me by talking of love, and then obstinately, with worrisome silence, says nothing about loving me. But yet, even though I learn it from someone else, I shall be happy to be the loved one.

A flattering breeze, "Hope," it tells me, "Hope! 39 You are the fair one"; but another one answers, confounding my happiness, "No, you are not the one." (*Exit, and* GERINA *starts to follow her.*)

Scene xix
MUSTAFÀ *and* GERINA

MUS. Pst, pst, a word. 40

GER. I have to go with my mistress.

MUS. And does your ladyship go off without bestowing a glance on me? You know quite well that I am tormented and on fire; but after you saw that little tailor's dummy, yes, I guess it, some devil has gotten into your head.

GER. (The occasion is ripe to make him despair.) To tell the truth, may it not displease you, that stranger attracts and pleases me a great deal.

MUS. (O Heavens!) And how, how could you stoop to looking favorably . . .

GER. Oh, this is nice! It is a habit of every woman to look with greater pleasure on a stranger than on her fellow citizen whom she always has around.

MUS. So, cruel girl, do you boast that you look with greater pleasure on that puny little body than on this fine figure of mine?

GER. Of course, and rightly so.

MUS. How come?

GER. Now I'll tell you. He is handsomer than you, more fit, more agile, and slenderer; he has greater grace in himself, and then too . . . he is more of a boy.

MUS. You make me angry by saying such mad things.

GER. Mad things? Show me the opposite.

MUS. Now I shall show you, without using either paint or ink: Look, what grace in walking! See, what affectation in looking! I am most handsome, lively, and light. Did you ever see such a leap? If you wish to decide between beauty and age, Gerina my dear, I have to laugh, for you are saying it to be funny, but not in earnest, or to make me now get angry.

GER. For what you have shown me, I care nothing at all, because a woman turns her tongue only where her tooth aches.

MUS. Yes, but she is always deceived, and loses all the rewards for her cleverness, because in the long run she always attaches herself to what is worst.

GER. That little face, so pretty, has wounded me, 41 pierced me with an arrow, nor do I care anymore for you. His eyes, so lively, are the torches which set fire to my heart and my heart swears faithfulness to him.

MUS. Yes, all of this is involved! (I can't stand it any 42 longer!) Gerina, now you will see what Mustafà can do. I want to gouge out those eyes which have pierced you with arrows; I want to tear out that heart which awoke passion in you. Your fair lover will fall at my feet torn in pieces, nor do I care if they impale me afterwards.

GER. Listen to me . . .

MUS. It must be thus.

GER. One word . . .

MUS. One word?

GER. One, yes; I ask no more.

MUS. Quickly, why are you delaying any longer?
GER. My darling, I love you.
MUS. You love me, hey?
GER. Certainly.
MUS. But that dandy?
GER. I shall never look at him again.
MUS. Gerina, you are deceiving me.
GER. Never fear.
MUS. And why thrash me with the cruel whip of jealously?
GER. Because I wanted, my soul, to discover from your sorrow whether your fair heart loves me.
MUS. And could you doubt . . .
GER. O Heavens! Don't you know? You're not the first man to betray women.
MUS. Yes, and women, too, don't do that sort of thing?
GER. Come now, no more; give me your hand.
MUS. Here it is.
GER. And let this hand draw the chains even tighter.
MUS. }I swear eternal faithfulness to you, my dearly
GER. }beloved.
43 MUS. My little Gerina—
GER. Mustafà.
MUS. You are clever.
MUS. Will you mock at me }
  any more like that? }No, my beloved, no, no,
GER. Will you believe me }nevermore.
  unfaithful? }
MUS. (To gain a fair woman one absolutely has to stay in slavery near her, night and day.)
GER. (A wise woman has to arouse jealously to keep her lover in slavery all the time.)

END OF ACT I

ACT II

Scene i

A courtyard connecting with the prison of the captives.
ERNESTO, *later* MUSTAFÀ.

44
45 ERN. A flattering hope has deceived me, and fate has armed itself with rigor. In vain, in vain I brought together the scattered ships to a lonely shore, if I still do not find Cunegonda.
MUS. (I still do not see that fop Ersindo.)
ERN. (That man, who by his appearance and bearing seems to be a court servant, perhaps may have some information concerning Ersindo.)
MUS. (Who can this man be?)
ERN. Friend, may Heaven preserve you.
MUS. Is your lordship speaking to me?
ERN. Precisely.
MUS. In what can I serve you?
ERN. May it not trouble you to tell me whether you know, among the captives, a certain Ridolfo.
MUS. Ridolfo? Most certainly, since I am the keeper of all the captives, and this certain Ridolfo is, among all of them, the dearest to me.
ERN. (O happy fortune!) Friend, if you allow me to speak with him, your favor will have a fitting reward.
MUS. Are you joking, my lord? I do not undertake out of self-interest to render a service to a person of your standing.

ERN. Take this.
MUS. What is it?
ERN. A little gold—not as a reward, but only as a small token of a grateful heart for your efforts. And if . . .
MUS. Say on.
ERN. And if you promise to free Ridolfo, to flee with me, you will have whatever you yearn for.
MUS. This is a kind of affair which cannot be touched so easily, because there is a very severe justice in Egypt.
ERN. What fear is there, if you can flee with us?
MUS. That is true; but I must think it over. For now, I can not promise it; but you remain around here, and I shall come back shortly to take you to Ridolfo.
ERN. I place my trust in you.
MUS. Farewell.
ERN. O happy me! But what will happen to Ridolfo, when I reveal to him the unfortunate loss of his faithful bride?
  If I conceal the death of the faithful lady, faith will   46
  complain of my deceit, and if I speak, it will make
  stronger the torment of the gyves.

Scene ii
MUSTAFA, *later* CUNEGONDÀ

MUS. If that man rewards me so well just for talking   47
  a little with Ridolfo, what will he do later if I give
  him freedom? Eh, this Ridolfo, I believe for sure,
  must be a great lord; and if I feel like it, I shall flee
  with him, and then I shall no longer be a poor man.
  But . . . Gerina's love? I shall take her along with me.
  No sir, no sir, it is a great mistake to trust women.
  Therefore I shall go alone, and shall satisfy my desires; he who has money will not lack for a wife.
  When you have money in your pocketbook, every   48
  woman bows to you and looks on you with an in-
  finity of favors. When you have such a key, every
  great door can be opened, and the whole world can
  indeed be turned topsy-turvy. But Ersindo is already   49
  coming. To whom do you wish to speak?
CUN. To Ridolfo of Germany.
MUS. I shall send him to you immediately. (*Exit.*)
CUN. If on this day Fate does not smile pityingly on
  me, I am done for.
  O just gods, give back to my heart that treasure, for   50
  which this faithful heart sighs, for the sorrow of my
  soul has become so fierce that it is too cruel. Just
  gods, give back to my heart . . .

Scene iii
CUNEGONDA *on one side and* RIDOLFO *on the other, issu-
ing forth from the great portal of the prison, followed
by guards.*

CUN. (Here is Ridolfo. Ah! I now recognize my delight,   51
  at the cost of the past peril.)
RID. Who is calling me from my fetters?
CUN. An unhappy person.
RID. Never so much so as I.
CUN. Perhaps more so.
CUN. He who is born under the same sky quickly con-
  curs harmoniously in feeling.
RID. From what country?
CUN. Bohemian.

198

RID. Birthplace of a woman, O Heavens all too faithless.

CUN. (Do I live thus in his heart, and still remain silent?) It seems that a greater trouble than that of the gyves is piercing your heart.

RID. Alas, unfortunately it is all too true.

CUN. I did not believe that there was any other suffering greater than captivity in this place.

RID. (Let him give me information about my faithless bride.) Perhaps Cunegonda is known to you.

CUN. As well as I am to myself.

RID. And you probably know the terrible story of the ill-fated loves of Prince Ridolfo.

CUN. As well as my own.

RID. But perhaps you do not know that I myself am that unhappy prince.

CUN. (I know it too well, alas, too well.) My lord, are you he?

RID. I, who have already been wearing these gyves for two years, am he.

CUN. Cruel fate!

RID. But what wounds my heart is that no word of Cunegonda has yet arrived here.

CUN. (And yet I tried to send many messages! Ah, I cannot resist.) Perhaps more than one letter has gone astray along the uncertain way.

RID. Do not flatter me. By this first embrace, in which I enfold you in sign of friendship, tell me whether Cunegonda is in the arms of someone else.

CUN. (You will die if I say that, and I if I am silent.)

RID. Speak. Ah! yes, I understand, Cunegonda is faithless, or else she is dead.

CUN. No, Prince, take comfort; she is a great deal more faithful than you desire her.

RID. What proof is there?

CUN. (Oh, what pain, to conceal the truth!) I plowed the waves with her, while the faithful girl came to Egypt to set you free.

RID. Cunegonda in Egypt?

CUN. At least I hope so.

RID. You did not come with her?

CUN. A fierce storm separated us before we landed on shore.

RID. And did she die in it?

CUN. It is well to hope that such faithfulness has been saved.

RID. Ah, she is dead. My fate is too, too hostile to me. I feel that her life is certainly in danger, which gives me more torment than does unfaithfulness.

52   You are dead, O loving bride, and your faithfulness killed you; but I wish to follow faithfully your shade with gyves on my feet.

CUN. I am not dead, O loving bridegroom; I tell it to you for her; I am living, and hope that one day the fetters will be stricken from your feet.

RID. You are ⎰
CUN. I am not ⎱ dead, etc.

Scene iv
CUNEGONDA, RIDOLFO, *and* ROSANA

53   RID. (Untimely arrival!)

ROS. Ersindo, is this the captive to whom you said you would unburden your heart?

CUN. (I wish it were not he!) It is he.

ROS. Have you told him your troubles yet?

CUN. He knew part of them. I told him a part, and a part I had to keep silent, because of a fatal consideration.

ROS. So you deceived me?

CUN. No, I said a great deal.

ROS. And let this be made known to me through his mouth.

RID. None of this is known to me.

ROS. You will be more wretched, if you are still silent.

CUN. Tell what you know, quickly.

RID. I do not know.

CUN. Do you not know how Prince Ridolfo stretched out his hands for chains instead of for a royal wedding?

ROS. What importance does Ridolfo have?

RID. (I am he.)

CUN. (And I am Cunegonda.) A great deal. And then did I not tell you that Love had brought faithful Cunegonda to shipwreck?

RID. (Too well, alas too well did you tell it.)

ROS. I am asking concerning your loves, not those of Cunegonda.

CUN. (And I am Cunegonda.)

ROS. I do not understand these unknown adventures, and if you hope to disappoint my desires with them, you hope in vain. Come, wretch. (*To* RIDOLFO) Let the secret promised to you, and owed to me, be drawn from that bosom. To work!

Scene v
CUNEGONDA, RIDOLFO, ROSANA, GERINA, *and* ALADINO

GER. Here is the sultan, my lady.   54

ROS. (O Heavens! What shall I say? At least let Ersindo be saved.)

ALA. My dear, what cloud of disdain is arising to darken your brow?

ROS. My lord, that base captive is guarding a secret too jealously.

GER. Oh, what bad manners!

ALA. And is it quite important?

ROS. He knows, O Sire, Ersindo's birthplace, adventures, and rank.

ALA. And does he dare to conceal them, and you are troubled thereby? (*To* RIDOLFO) Speak immediately!

CUN. Ah, in vain you seek for what the unhappy man does not know. I shall tell it (before my beloved is endangered).

ROS. Be silent! (If Ersindo speaks, I am exposed.) (*To* CUNEGONDA) You might be lying; I want to know it from him.

ALA. Speak, then; why are you delaying?

RID. And what knowledge is desired?

ALA. Concerning Ersindo . . .

ROS. Ah, Sire, to me . . . (If the sultan inquires any further, I am in danger.) What is desired, villain? What you have been guilty of concealing so far.

RID. I have already said that I know nothing.

ALA. And do you still resist?

CUN. (Ah, what suffering is mine!)

ALA. Let the secret be drawn out of that fellow's bosom

by torture, and then if he still refuses, let him be executed.

ROS. No, no, let me tempt that heart in a calmer way; flattery may bring out of him some secret, which death might bury with him.

ALA. As you wish, Rosana, just so as you are appeased. (*To* RIDOLFO) You take counsel of the danger which is near; if you do not wish to speak, peril is certain. (*To* ROSANA) If I see in that face the flash of a smile, severity departs; you are smiling, my fair one. (*To* RIDOLFO) You, wretch, tremble, for the flash still foretells the thunderbolt.

Scene vi

ROSANA, RIDOLFO, CUNEGONDA, GERINA, *and later* MUSTAFÀ

ROS. (I breathe again, O gods!) Do you see that being silent may cost him his life? Do you see it, Ersindo? Delay no longer; if you wish him safe, speak, and if you wish him dead, be silent.

GER. Ersindo, delay speech no longer, and then, believe me, you can do whatever you wish. (ROSANA *and* GERINA *go aside.*)

RID. Did you promise?

CUN. I promised.

RID. Promise is duty.

CUN. Ah, if you knew the object of my love you would be the first to be strong in silence, for a flame when hidden is torment, when revealed it is danger.

ROS. (*To* GERINA, *aside*) To love me is indeed a risk.

GER. And this is certain.

RID. Then what is to be promised?

CUN. I did not ever foresee so many witnesses, and so many obstacles.

RID. Is your flame known to the one who kindled it?

CUN. I have said so much, that I believe my constancy and my faithfulness are obvious.

ROS. (*To* GERINA) (And for me he has said a great deal.)

GER. Oh, most certainly.

RID. What is keeping you from speaking more freely?

CUN. Because I find my beloved surrounded by guards and keepers.

ROS. (*To* GERINA) (What he says is for me.)

GER. (There is no doubt any longer.)

RID. What does it matter whether strangers' loves are known to the common folk of the Nile?

CUN. Because my beloved is in their power.

ROS. (What more, my faithful girl? I am such.)

GER. (It is certain, yes, most certain.)

RID. These delays, my friend, strengthen the arm of the powerful and resolute woman.

CUN. Do not seek a secret which, while it is concealed, is of no concern to you (ROSANA *comes forth, furious, and* GERINA *remains aside.*)

ROS. If it is of no concern to him, it is to Rosana. The chains of this madman, who does not reveal a secret, shall be doubled, and they shall be put on this one, who was not willing for it to be revealed.

CUN. Since it is insisted on by force, and that same penalty is prescribed for silence as for revealing the object of my love (*to* RIDOLFO) tell her that my beloved is present, and that you are the one.

RID. (To Rosana?)

ROS. I am not satisfied any longer. Ho there! (GERINA *comes forward.*)

MUS. Here I am.

ROS. Let these two be taken to the royal baths, separately from each other.

MUS. I shall do as you command.

ROS. (There, less in the public eye and without obstacles, I shall assure myself more of his love.)

GER. (What more do you desire, fair lady? It seems to me that he is speaking quite clearly.)

ROS. I feel my heart in my bosom shining, nor do I know why; Love, thou knowest. Who knows, but what as a reward for my intense pains I shall have as great enjoyment as I have had sorrow? (*Exit.*)

Scene vii

RIDOLFO, CUNEGONDA, MUSTAFÀ, *and* GERINA

MUS. (*To some of the soldiers*) I entrust Ridolfo to you; take him to the baths. (*To another group of soldiers*) And let it be your concern to take Ersindo; but make sure that the two of them never speak to each other. (MUSTAFÀ *goes aside to observe* GERINA.)

RID. I must leave you, and yet I still do not know what is the fate of my Cunegonda.

GER. (Oh, this is really too much! With so much embarrassment as Mustafà causes me, I am going to make him really despair.) (*She sets herself to observing* ERSINDO.)

RID. I return } to chains,
CUN. You return }

RID. But first tell me . . .

CUN. Nor can I tell you . . .

RID. Where is the treasure of my } heart.
CUN. I am the treasure of your }

(Oh, could I at least tell him that my heart says to him: Farewell all faith and all love.)

Scene viii

GERINA *and* MUSTAFÀ

GER. (Ersindo is already leaving; I am going to follow him, to cause Mustafà even greater pain.)

MUS. Gerina, where are you going?

GER. Where I feel like. This is a nice how-de-do! Do I have to render an account to you for every step I take?

MUS. Certainly, and I've stopped you, because you were following Ersindo.

GER. And I shall follow Ersindo.

MUS. Stop, traitress. Tell me: don't you know that it's not proper for you, who have promised me your faith and love, to follow someone else?

GER. Eh! I don't need good humor. So much haughtiness is of no use to me. I am not your slave, and I too can be bold. I am not frightened at your words; and when I want to, I shall know how to overcome so much pride.

MUS. You're a woman, what can I say? If you were a man, you'd see . . .

GER. And what would I see? Oh, oh, Mr. High-and-Mighty, you don't know, you don't know. If I want, I'll have you . . . I'll have you . . .

MUS. Tell me, what will you have done to me . . . ?

GER. I'll have you beaten.

MUS. Take it easy, Sir Roland. Me!

GER. Yes, yes, you'll see.

MUS. Eh! I am never frightened of women.

63 GER. Listen . . .

MUS. Softly!

GER. You don't believe . . .

MUS. What?

GER. If you don't see . . .

MUS. What?

GER. That you will be . . .

MUS. What?

GER. The object of my anger, the object of my fury.

MUS. Ah, ah, my Gerina, I laugh at your fury. I am not afraid of your disdain . . .

GER. (Enough, enough, you'll see.)

MUS. For my bosom . . .

GER. (You'll become aware of it.)

MUS. Never knew fear.

GER. (. . . if I make you feel fear.)

Scene ix
Thermal establishment with baths. ROSANA, ARSACE.

64 ROS. Frenzies of love, you will soon be calmed; but the more impatient is my flame, the more jealous it grows. Since it has been revealed to that captive, let him be done away with before he informs anyone else of it.

ARS. Queen, at your orders.

ROS. Listen to me, Arsace. That European captive who has been brought to the baths by the servants . . .

ARS. I have seen him.

ROS. He must be guarded with jealous care, until there arises some fitting occasion to have him killed.

ARS. In a palace, where Fate often dwells, it will not be difficult to find a pretext for his death.

ROS. As important as my greatness and your command. He is in possession of a secret which, if revealed, imperils us both.

ARS. I shall guard him watchfully, nor shall I have him brought forth from the gates except to go to his death.

65 If innocence makes itself an enemy, it sometimes earns a death-sentence. That slaughter which defends a throne overcomes the strength of justice. (*Exit.*)

Scene x
ROSANA, *seated; enter* CUNEGONDA

66 ROS. (Here is my beloved.)

CUN. (What will be my fate?)

ROS. (And yet he shyly avoids looking at me. Let the new lover be given courage.) Ersindo?

CUN. (*Kneels*) Here I am at your feet; but first I beg you that Ersindo's guilt, which up to now has been hidden, should not be extended to make others unhappy.

ROS. Stand up, for my consent forgives you, also for having spoken. Even a royal love, when it is pleasing, goes without guilt to whomsoever may aid it.

CUN. (Royal love? How is it known to Rosana?)

ROS. Sit with me.

CUN. I should sit? (What kind of beginning is this?)

ROS. Do not become confused, because by saying it your misdemeanour loses its unseemliness.

CUN. (What meaning has this? I begin to suspect some hidden deception in Rosana.)

ROS. Sit here with me, my dear.

CUN. (My doubts become certainty.)

ROS. More than your love, your coldness is at fault.

CUN. (Shall I disclose myself? The presumptuous woman will be indignant.)

ROS. Come, my heart; do not be frightened of the lightning bolts of royal majesty, for love has suppressed them.

CUN. (Let her dawning love be cut short in its cradle.)

ROS. Why are you delaying any longer?

CUN. Madam, I desire to see you freed of misunderstanding, and myself of torment. I should like to see clipped the wings of a love which has been born without hope.

ROS. Those traitorous lips said they loved me.

CUN. Did I ever say I loved you?

ROS. Behold the innocent! Did you not tell Ridolfo that your beloved was present?

CUN. I did.

ROS. Was there any other woman there?

CUN. There was not.

ROS. And did you then add, turning to me, that I was that woman?

CUN. I did not speak to you.

ROS. You are lying, you wretch. You are guilty of having, through deceit, brought forth from my unwary heart a love which, when not reciprocated, is mad.

CUN. A lowly foreigner . . .

ROS. My affection made you very great.

CUN. I would not be guilty . . .

ROS. Close your lips, you villain.

CUN. I obey.

ROS. A loving flame which has been despised admits no excuses.
On the altar of vengeance I shall sacrifice this unhappy love; lightning, thunder, and arrows shall fall upon the traitor. 67

Scene xi
CUNEGONDA

CUN. Cunegonda, you feared lest speaking harm you; 68 but you find, on the contrary, that your silence was harmful to you. The secret of your sex is still kept, hiding it even from your Ridolfo; but this fatal mistake will then double his shackles with yours.
You alone have deluded fair hope—fatal deceit! The 69 constancy of the heart is already languishing, betrayed with a mortal wound.

Scene xii
ERNESTO *and* RIDOLFO

ERN. Such is, O Prince, the faithfulness of your 70 Cunegonda; but her fate is as uncertain as her constancy is certain.

RID. And why abandon her?

ERN. She was safer in the shelter than on the bosom of the waves.

RID. And did the shepherd give you no more information concerning my faithful bride?

ERN. After she left with me, he saw her no more.

RID. Go in search of her, and use just as much of every art to find my bride as you use cautiously for my liberty.

ERN. But first let us get out of these shackles, for the guardian is already prepared, with gifts and flattery, for my entry into the baths and your flight.

RID. Do not speak of freedom until you bring news to me either of her life or of her death.

Scene xiii
ARSACE, RIDOLFO, ERNESTO

71 ARS. (To RIDOLFO) Stay your footsteps, wretch.

ARS. (To ERNESTO) And you, why by your face and your unusual garb are clearly a foreigner, how did you dare to enter within these walls?

ERN. (What shall I say?) The desire to admire such a vast building impelled me.

ARS. (The opportunity of getting rid of that fellow is already presenting itself.) (To RIDOLFO) He who comes to admire is not concerned with consorting with captives. You both attempted a prearranged flight, and you are both guilty.

ERN. Escapes are not arranged among servants and guardians.

RID. The foreigner was born in my country.

ARS. The crime is all the more sure because of that. But is the sultan here? Let him know their guilt, and decree an appropriately severe penalty for their daring.

Scene xiv
ARSACE, RIDOLFO, ERNESTO, and ALADINO

72 RID. (Ah, we are lost, Ernesto.)

ALA. What is this dispute, Arsace?

ARS. You arrive on time, Your Majesty, to punish a great crime.

ALA. Are these the guilty ones?

ARS. They are.

ALA. Who is that man?

ARS. A foreigner who came to profane the royal dwelling. The other is Ridolfo, chosen for the service of the royal baths, and with him he was concocting hidden schemes and planning flight.

ALA. Did you dare to do so much, risking punishment, wretch?

ERN. Your Majesty, it is not the fault . . .

RID. Silence, Ernesto, for there is no defense against tyranny.

ALA. A crime in which the criminal takes pleasure becomes all the greater.

RID. And let the guilty one be given greater punishment; but let your wrath be content with only one victim, O king. Death is my due, but he is innocent.

ALA. Death to you, death to him, death to whoever is an accomplice in the attempted escape. (Pointing to RIDOLFO) Arsace, let him be destined in the royal gardens for the pleasure of our blows. (Pointing to ERNESTO) Let every secret be wrung from him by means of torture. If he remain obdurate, let him die immediately, a victim of my wrath. (Exit.)

Scene xv
ARSACE, RIDOLFO, ERNESTO, and later MUSTAFÀ

ARS. Let the foreigner follow me. Ho there!   73

MUS. My lord, what is your wish?

ARS. Let the captive be led by the soldiers to his execution in the royal gardens. (Exit.)

MUS. I shall obey your orders.

ERN. Sir, I leave you, and shall die happy if I am allowed to join my last breath with yours.

RID. Cunegonda, you are waiting for me on the banks   74
of Lethe, whither I send a sigh as a harbinger of my coming.

My suffering is consoled by this hope alone, of   75
joining you, adored shade, in the Elysian Fields. Beloved, if I lost you, you are my death, but a death more blessed than life.

Scene xvi
MUSTAFÀ, and later GERINA with a slave with a saber and a club in his hand.

MUS. You follow him still to the royal garden; there let   76
him be kept, and wait for me. Mustafà, give a little thought to your affairs. Here we are dealing with madmen. That insane girl met you a short while ago without giving you a greeting, and yet another time she threatened you. Yes, with your bravery something fearful might still happen to you!

Every leaf which moves makes me suddenly afraid;   77
it seems that my heart and my lungs are no longer in their places. Mustafà, Gerina said it to you and is doing it to you.

But this is cowardice. Let whoever wishes come, I   78
will fight with death. Now let us go to the garden. (As he is going in, he meets GERINA with the slave, and makes an about-face.) (Woe is me!)

GER. Hey, sir!

MUS. (Now I'm for it!) I am your most humble servant. My fairest Gerina, have pity on me; I had not seen you, for otherwise I would have done part of my more than greatest duty.

GER. (Oh, what a pleasure it is to frighten him!) Eh, all this ceremony is of no use. I am here to show you that I am a most punctual woman, and what I have promised you, I am now most ready to see to it.

MUS. What did you promise me? I remember nothing, in truth.

GER. That fellow with his club will tell you.

MUS. (Bad!) Eh! I know you're joking. Does it seem fitting to you that an official of my rank should undergo . . .

GER. The club, yes, sir. (To the slave) Now is the time.

MUS. (What am I to do?) At least . . .

GER. It is not to be so any longer. (To the slave) Go to it!

MUS. Take it easy, take it easy. (O woe is me!) Only jealousy . . .

GER. (I'm dying with laughter!)

MUS. . . . made me get angry . . .

GER. (He's trembling from head to foot.)

MUS. Besides, it's you . . .

GER. Silence, wretch, and don't talk to me any more.
Come, come, my beloved, no, don't be afraid, show   79
courage; what does this trembling mean? Didn't I tell you that you were to be the object and target of my anger, of my wrath?

MUS. (Mustafà, what are you doing? Are you appearing base?) Eh! Madam Gerina, these threats don't frighten me, for a man like me isn't afraid; but it is not fitting for a soldier to use a club.

GER. In this, yes, you're right; but that man is a soldier, too, and he will fight you with a sword.

MUS. (What the devil tempted you?) I am ready.

GER. Then to arms! (*The slave throws away the club and draws his sword.*)

MUS. No, no, because now I have to go to the garden.

GER. No excuses are allowed.

MUS. Tomorrow, at break of day, I shall return here.

GER. If you don't fight now, I shall declare you a coward.

MUS. (What shall I do?) I, a coward?

GER. If you don't fight, he'll use the club.

MUS. (Ah woe is me, what confusion!) Here I am ready.

GER. (*To the slave*) Go to it! (MUSTAFÀ *starts to draw his swords, and stops.*)

MUS. Ow, ow!

GER. What's the matter?

MUS. A certain cramp, which often comes to me in this shoulder, gives me a bad pain.

GER. Say, rather, that you have no courage.

MUS. I have no courage? Powers of the world... (MUSTAFÀ *draws his saber, and, on starting to stand on his guard, stops.*)

MUS. Ow, ow!

GER. What's up? Perhaps you have another flimsy excuse?

MUS. I've just gotten an attack of podagra.

GER. This kind of babbling is useless. If you don't fight now, I'll have you slain.

MUS. Softly, softly, good fellow!

GER. (What fun!)

MUS. (And is there not even a dog, to come and prevent this duel?)

GER. Come, to arms; no need of delaying any further.

MUS. With all my pain, I shall try it. (*The duel follows, and* MUSTAFÀ *falls and is left without his sword.*)

MUS. Have mercy, have mercy!

GER. Beg me for your life.

MUS. Grant me my life, for pity's sake!

GER. It shall be granted you; but learn, another time, to be in good humor.

MUS. I shall not do it any more. (A curse upon love!)

GER. (*To the slave*) My good man, go away; I shall reward you for your kind help.

MUS. May heaven bring a murrain on him to be his reward!

81 I swear to Heaven that if another time I meet up with your blusterer, I shall cut him into pieces, hack him up, flay him, for I am not afraid of him.

GER. Sir Boaster, listen, hear me; stop for a little bit; now I shall call him back, and you can fight with him, since you are such a sure blade.

MUS. Now I am so crippled, I don't feel up to fighting.

GER. You are crippled in your brain, because you are pretending to limp.

MUS. Do you know why I didn't slay him? I respected your presence, because on seeing him die you might have fainted on seeing so much blood.

GER. Thanks so much for the favor, because for sure

I have so tender a heart of pulp that just a little bit of blood is enough to make me fall in a faint.

END OF ACT II

ACT III

Scene i

Royal garden with tent, under which the sultan is to sit. ROSANA, GERINA, *and later* ARSACE.

ROS. Sad, despised love, I am not going to listen to you weeping. 82

GER. Oh, there's no need for so many laments, madam; you must divert yourself, and believe me, enjoyment is no shame. 83

ARS. Rosana, Fate is favorable to your wish. The occasion has already arisen, and the hated captive is near to his fated death.

ROS. And do you think, then, that with only that death you have assured the throne of Egypt for me, and the command for yourself?

ARS. Is there any obstacle remaining?

ROS. O Heavens! I fear so. That foreign youth is too highly esteemed.

ARS. And what power has a base lad today in Egypt?

ROS. A great deal over a fickle heart, and more over the sultan.

ARS. A vain and useless thought.

GER. The sultan and Ersindo are alone in the garden.

ARS. I shall not fear as long as your love, O my sister, is on the throne. (*Exit.*)

Scene ii
ROSANA *and* GERINA

ROS. Eh, if you are imprudent, I am not a fool. Let the footsteps of the king and of the foreigner not be lost from sight, until my vengeance falls on the guilty one. Let every thought and every word be scanned. Let him not be given time to reveal my mistake; he who is first to accuse, even if he is not innocent, at least seems so. 84

In the cold blast of vengeance the god of Love falls dead; and from this alone my sad heart hopes for some peace. (*Goes aside.*) 85

GER. Oh, how much my mistress knows! She is clever, she is shrewd, she is canny; but among all women, she is not the only one to be that way. I am greatly afraid for my dear Ersindo, for Hell hath no fury like a woman scorned. 86

In my bosom my palpitating heart is trembling, and for that unfortunate lad I feel a shiver which almost, almost makes me faint. O Heavens! Would that he had never come here! Or would that I had never known him, for then I would not have such dread sufferings. (*Goes aside to where* ROSANA *is.*) 87

Scene iii
ALADINO, CUNEGONDA, *and* MUSTAFÀ

ALA. To the charms of Flora, where I often come down to relax from the cares of ruling, add the harmony of your songs, Ersindo. See to it, in short, that I rest, with your singing over my sleep, at the foot of the throne; for the repose of the great is not relaxation. 88

MUS. (Oh, what good luck! I want to stand here, meanwhile, to listen to Ersindo's singing.) (Goes aside; CUNEGONDA sings, while ALADINO stretches out on cushions under the tent.)

89 CUN. Beautiful rose, hope, hope that you will soon have your beauty back. Even if an ungrateful evening took from you your greatness and your beauty, at the return of a fresh dawn the south wind will become friendly again.

90 Thus was a faithful lover in the habit of singing cheerfully about her captive beloved's chains. With the milk of hope, she either softened her grief or kept her constancy alive. The unfortunate girl was already stretching out her right hand to at least lighten his chains, when, oh fatal event! a tyrannical woman, on account of an ill-conceived love, divided them both and killed a newborn hope.

Scene iv

ALADINO, CUNEGONDA, MUSTAFÀ, ROSANA, and ARSACE

91 ROS. (Aside) Let this speech, disastrous to Rosana, be cut short, Arsace. Whether the king is sleeping or not, awaken him immediately. (Withdraws.)

MUS. (He sang very well, though!)

CUN. (Rosana here!)

ARS. My lord, the captive, destined to the honor of your blows, awaits your royal orders.

ALA. Enough, Ersindo. (To MUSTAFA) Let him be brought for the fated purpose.

MUS. I shall now have him brought in. (Wretched Ridolfo!) (Exit.)

ALA. (To CUNEGONDA) Ersindo, I challenge your heart to a new assault. You promised me to be bold at the sight of death. Now let us see whether your bravery will keep your promises, for there is no room for fear in the vicinity of a king.

92 Ersindo, be courageous, ah, abandon fear. Consider the rose, which is blood-colored to make itself more agreeable for our pleasure.

Scene v

ALADINO, CUNEGONDA, MUSTAFÀ, ROSANA, and ARSACE. RIDOLFO is led in by soldiers with his hands tied behind his back.

93 MUS. Here he is. (To soldiers) Tie him well to that tree trunk. (And yet I am sorry for him!)

CUN. (Ridolfo here, bound? Ah, what fearful way is this, O Heavens!, of leading innocent men?)

ALA. Let a bow and arrow be brought. (Exit MUSTAFÀ, and return with the bow and arrow; RIDOLFO is tied to a tree.)

RID. (Here is, finally, that death which I formerly desired so as to flee the faithless woman, and now is granted me so as to follow the faithful shade.)

MUS. Here is the bow and the arrow.

ALA. Give them to Ersindo. (MUSTAFÀ gives the bow and arrow to CUNEGONDA.)

CUN. For what purpose, my lord?

ALA. Do you see that condemned man?

CUN. (I see him, I recognize him, and what a sight!)

ALA. Direct the shot at that audacious man's bosom, with great wounds.

CUN. (For me it is the greatest shot that death sharpens.)

ALA. For you the honor of the first arrow, Ersindo.

CUN. (And does Cunegonda suffer even to be tempted?)

ALA. Why are you delaying?

CUN. (What way out is there?) My untrained right hand does not know how to fit the arrow to the bow. (ALADINO takes the bow from CUNEGONDA's hand and pretends to shoot.)

ALA. Look, first you fit the arrow onto the bow, and then bending the stem like this . . . (CUNEGONDA takes the bow from ALADINO's hand.)

CUN. Enough, I have already learned.

RID. (They are arguing there over my wounds.)

MUS. (He moves me to pity.)

ALA. Let's see.

CUN. (I shall break the arrow in this bosom.) (Tries to wound herself.) (But the tyrant is not lacking for other arrows.)

ALA. Why so slow?

CUN. I am practising my hand. (CUNEGONDA pretends to try to shoot.)

ALA. Bend the bow.

CUN. It is ready. (Oh gods, what torture!)

ALA. Shoot the arrow. (CUNEGONDA relaxes the bow and drops her arm.)

CUN. My arm has no strength left. (Oh, my Ridolfo!)

RID. Hasten the blow, friend.

ALA. You are really cowardly, Ersindo. (ALADINO takes the bow from CUNEGONDA.)

MUS. (Now he's really done for.)

Scene vi

ALADINO, CUNEGONDA, and MUSTAFÀ. ROSANA comes forth with ARSACE and GERINA.

ARS. (What are you thinking, my sister?)

ROS. (You shall see now.)

CUN. (The hit is certain.) Ah, my lord . . . (ALADINO lifts up the bow to shoot RIDOLFO.)

ROS. My lord, turn your wrath upon a better object.

ALA. What troubles you, my dearest?

ROS. Your offended honor calls for vengeance.

ALA. And I promise vengeance. Point out the culprit to me.

ROS. There he is. Your Ersindo, who has been raised so high in your royal favor.

ALA. You, the culprit?

CUN. Both the accusation and the guilt are strange to me.

MUS. (Oh, here is another fine mess!)

ROS. Listen to such innocence! Certainly the offended one will blush more to tell it, than the daring guilty one did in committing it.

ALA. Delay no longer, Rosana.

ROS. The reckless one—ah, I am pained in telling it!—the reckless fellow dared to tempt my faithfulness.

ALA. And were you so daring, you wretch, and so base?

CUN. I neither dreamed nor could I dream of such an offense.

ROS. It is useless for you to deny it; there is proof of your crime.

CUN. The proof will be like the accusation.

ROS. Let the captive be unbound, who was present at a large part of your misdemeanor; let him tell of it. (MUSTAFÀ has RIDOLFO unbound.)

MUS. Quick, quick, let him be released. (Ridolfo, be of good cheer, for now your fate is delayed. Have hope, perhaps, who knows?)

RID. (I am taken to a different death, or to a worse life.)

CUN. (And can Ridolfo do this?)

ROS. Come, wretch, and answer my questions truthfully. Did you ask this person, at my command, what was the object of his love?

RID. I do not deny it.

ROS. Did he not answer you boldly, "Tell her that my beloved is present"?

RID. This, too, is true.

ROS. Did you see any other woman?

RID. I saw no other.

ROS. Did he not add to me later that I was she?

RID. He did not speak to me.

CUN. (To RIDOLFO) I spoke to you. Your Majesty, it is all deceit.

ALA. Your crime has no defense.

MUS. (The wretch is convicted; oh, what pity I feel for him!)

GER. (O Heavens, reveal the deception.)

RID. (I, a proof of his guilt? Alas, I am tormented by it.)

ALA. What more enormous outrage could you dream of, you audacious fellow? So that wicked right hand, which does not know how to shoot an arrow, knows how to injure fearlessly the reputation of a king?

CUN. (Ah, if my risk is able to save my beloved, let my sex remain concealed.) What do you demand of me? I am guilty and deserving of death.

ALA. And death you shall have. Arsace, let the bold fellow be pinned with a hundred arrows to a tree.

ARS. I shall obey.

ROS. (I am completely avenged.)

GER. (I feel my heart bursting. I shall leave so as not to see it.) (Exit.)

94 MUS. (He moves me to tears.) (Exit.)

CUN. (If Ridolfo does not die, it will be a lucky hit!) I shall die, cruel man; but my dead body will immediately cry out at the foot of your throne that you have been deceived, that I am not guilty.

95 CUN. (To ALADINO) You are condemning me as guilty, and I am not guilty.

ALA. Your guilt is too clear; die, evil wretch, traitor. (Exit.)

CUN. (To ROSANA) You accuse me of guilt, but I am not guilty.

ROS. For a love which lays the blame on the great, this is the way the despiser dies. (Exit.)

CUN. (To RIDOLFO) You caused me to be condemned, and I pardon you.

RID. The proof of your innocence, unfortunate one, is my grief.

Scene vii
CUNEGONDA, RIDOLFO, and ARSACE

RID. (But what will happen to me?)

ARS. (To CUNEGONDA) Make haste to your punishment, wretch.

CUN. You might better say, Arsace, the innocent victim to the sacrifice.

ARS. You do not seem like one.

CUN. And yet I am one. But I ask, not justice, which I

did not ask of the king, but a favor of you.

ARS. (I feel pity for him.) You shall have it, if it is such that it lies within my power.

CUN. I ask to speak with that captive. A favor is never denied to condemned wretches in their last moments.

ARS. I grant it, but let it be short. The king's disfavor admits of no delay to his vengeance. (Exit.)

Scene viii
CUNEGONDA and RIDOLFO

CUN. Prince, before dying, I wish to speak to you.

RID. Speak, unfortunate one, for if this is news of Cunegonda, you owe it to me.

CUN. It is unhappy news concerning Cunegonda.

RID. So she is dead? I asked once before, and you concealed it out of pity.

CUN. Would that she were dead, so that she would not now bring you the sorrow of seeing her die.

RID. What are you saying, fellow?

CUN. It is no longer time to conceal Cunegonda's identity. I am she.

RID. You, Cunegonda? Ah, what a name! Ah, what a sight! Ah, what a fate! Do I find you in this condition, my beloved, and recognize you? Say, why did you conceal it from me?

CUN. When you were revealed as yourself, my treasure, I was afraid of making your shackles heavier; and I feared my sex would expose me to licentious advances.

RID. Why keep it secret when accused unfairly? And why do you want to die, when you are innocent?

CUN. To save you, my dear heart.

RID. Ah, you are hoping to do so in vain, because cruel Aladino already wishes me dead.

CUN. He will quench his thirst for blood wholly in my bosom.

RID. If you are my soul, you are my life. Live for yourself, live for your people, live for your kingdom.

CUN. Let me die, and you flee; for if you save yourself, I shall die happy.

RID. Without you, my beloved soul, I despise kingdom, liberty, and life.

CUN. } Live, my beloved, for me it is enough.   96
RID. }

CUN. To make known to you my } faithfulness.
RID. To know your }

CUN. } Your love in vain contends for me to live without
RID. } you.

CUN. Here is Ernesto; let him show you the road to liberty. Is he coming between guards?

RID. The faithful man is coming to die.

CUN. For what crime?

RID. Knowing Ridolfo is his only crime.

CUN. When was he at the court? Has he placed the ships in safety? But why ask? We are all done for.

Scene ix
CUNEGONDA, and RIDOLFO. ERNESTO is led in by guards.

ERN. Princess, are you safe? And Ridolfo with you?

RID. Ernesto, you find us both unhappy.

ERN. Our Cunegonda is by herself enought to make you happy.

205

RID. Alas! I find her and I lose her.

ERN. Through what destiny?

CUN. Through a fatal deception. Rosana tempted me with love, and now the wicked woman, guilty of her mad error, drives me to death.

ERN. And because you hid from her that you are a woman.

CUN. To save my beloved, I was willing to be considered guilty.

RID. Ridolfo will not deny it.

CUN. If you snatch me from death, you leave me a victim of the sultan's lechery.

ERN. This is an uncertain evil; death is a certain one.

CUN. But it would be the worst of all evils.

ERN. One should flee from an evil which is sure, for Heaven will take care of what is uncertain.

CUN. No more; leave me to my fate. The soldiers nearby are signaling me to depart.

97   Ridolfo, farewell. If you remain alive, as a pledge of my love take my kingdom, and bring word back to my fatherland that Cunegonda died to save you.

98   Remember me, my life, farewell. The faith which I pledged to you I kept in constancy for you, even unto dying for you, my idol. (*Exit.*)

Scene x

ARSACE, RIDOLFO, ERNESTO

ARS. Keep him according to my orders, and take him to the nearby park, soldiers. (*To* RIDOLFO *and* ERNESTO) You too go to your final destiny?

RID. (Why hesitate any longer?) (*To* ARSACE) Let wrath thunder, O Arsace, but it is hurled in vain against that unfortunate person. First of all you should know that the crime, of which Rosana accused Ersindo, Rosana is guilty of.

ARS. Who could prove it?

RID. Everyone to whom it is known that Ersindo is a woman.

ARS. A woman, Ersindo? And she kept it a secret? And you are saying so?

ERN. I, who am of her retinue, I confirm it.

RID. I did not say so before because she still kept it a secret from me. There is no need of proofs where the facts are convincing. Nor can you fear that I am lying. The innocent defendant is in your power, and the liar in fetters.

ARS. If this is true, the severity of the law grows all the greater against her, because she makes Rosana guilty, and also against you, who knew it.

RID. So great an injustice will not remain hidden.

ARS. You will die, and the secret will be buried with you.

ERN. But its memory will not be lost on that account. She has ships and people in Egypt who, if they cannot obtain her safety, will seek vengeance.

RID. The sultan will know that Ersindo is a royal lady, able to arm a world against Egypt. He will know that love drew her, accompanied by armed men, to the sands of Africa

99   to bring back to the throne her beloved Ridolfo, Prince of Germany, and I am he.

100   My blood will cry out, stained with wrath and anger, for slaughter and vengeance. I shall make war, as a neglected shade, a bloodless corpse, on the Egyptian traitor. (*Exit.*)

ERN. Yes, the betrayed shades will cry out for vengeance to avenging Heaven; but because tyranny does not fear the gods, let it at least be afraid of the revenge that all the friendly kingdoms will bring with avenging swords one day against Africa.   101

Against Egypt Heaven and earth will take up arms. The unconquered Danube will challenge the Nile to war. (*Exit.*)   102

Scene xi

ARSACE, *later* MUSTAFÀ

ARS. My faithful followers, let each one of them be guarded in the most secret part of the park. They shall all have an unobserved death. But what are you saying, Arsace? Think, first, that with them Rosana's sin cannot die. The flight of the accused is the only thing that can preserve us. This is my resolve. Ho there!   103

MUS. My lord, what do you command?

ARS. Take those captives to the port, where the ships are shining with torches, in the approaching night, for my victories. There an armed boat of my warriors shall serve as an escort for them to their ships, and you wait for me there.

MUS. (O lucky me!) I shall carry out your orders. (I want to go with them, and Gerina and love can go to blazes.) (*Exit.*)

ARS. Often a heart seems rebellious, and is faithful. It is right to be afraid of cruel tyranny. (*Exit.*)   104

Scene xii

GERINA, *and then* MUSTAFÀ *in woman's clothing*

GER. To despise love is indeed a great folly! That wretch Ersindo—I'm still madly in love with him—is to be shot through with arrows, for having despised my mistress's love. Now I am not so hardhearted but that on occasion, if I see someone who has affection for me, if I could, I would take him to my bosom.   105

I laugh and joke with everybody, nor do I ever act bashful. Now I give this one a little grin, now I make a snappy wisecrack to that one; but love has not yet found a place in my heart. And that this is true, Mustafà can make it known, who proved it.   106

Oh, oh! What great high-sided vessel is this sailing into my presence? By that big fat body and by his appearance, it looks like Mustafà. But—yes, if I am not mistaken—it is indeed he. Now do you see that big fat booby? What in Heaven's name is he doing in those clothes? I shall withdraw here to one side to hear in secret what the mess is. (*Goes aside.*)   107

MUS. Oh! what a devilish nuisance it is to act like a woman! I have been in danger of falling at least five or six times on account of this skirt. (GERINA *comes near him.*) If I were to meet Gerina, she certainly would not recognize me! (GERINA *passes in front of him, looking him in the face.*)

MUS. (Didn't I say that she didn't know me?)

GER. Mustafà?

MUS. (Oh, the deuce!) (*Starts to go off.*)

206

GER. Where are you going? (MUSTAFA *starts to exit in another direction, and* GERINA *stands in his way again.*) Stop!

MUS. (I am discovered!) Who are you speaking to?

GER. To you. Do you think, perhaps, that you're not recognized?

MUS. Eh, let me go, for now I have things to do . . .

GER. First tell me why you are dressed up as a woman.

MUS. I can't tell you.

GER. But yet . . . ?

MUS. Other times, other cares.

GER. Ah, deceiver! (I want to discover his purpose.) Certainly this is a stratagem of love.

MUS. (What do I hear? He who feels jealousy has his heart wounded.)

GER. Ah, unfair one! Ah, thankless man! Is this the faith that you promised me?

MUS. (I am certainly not deceived; that proverb is not wrong, that love can never remain concealed.)

GER. You should not have wounded me, if you wanted to leave me.

MUS. (What shall I do? Shall I tell her? Don't betray me, Love.)

GER. You cruel man!

MUS. Listen, my heart; but you must promise silence.

GER. I promise it.

MUS. Because, scorned by you, I had decided to flee just now, with certain captives.

GER. (What do I hear!) And who are they?

MUS. Ridolfo, Ersindo, and Ernesto.

GER. Ah, disloyal man! Ah, faithless man! And you wanted to desert me?

MUS. You were the cause of this, by despising me. Only you, my fair Gerina, are my morning star, my moon, and my sun. Whether by night or by day I want to be around you because you are my consolation.

GER. (Now I'll console you, because I'll reveal everything to my mistress.) Now what are you thinking of doing?

MUS. Gerina dear, now I shall see whether you love me.

GER. What do you want?

MUS. I have undertaken to go with those captives, who have promised me bountiful wealth. Now if you . . .

GER. Come on, speak.

MUS. If you want to flee with me, we can enjoy a fine rest with our wealth.
And you will be my bride, and I your bridegroom.

GER. I am content; and when shall we go, my treasure?

MUS. Right now.

GER. Oh, what great joy! And where shall I meet you, my beloved?

MUS. I shall wait for you at the great port. Will you come, my fair treasure?

GER. Yes, my delight.

108 MUS. Come quickly, for my heart cannot exist far from you.

GER. Yes, I shall come, my sweet love. (I shall know how to put you well to scorn.)

MUS. What pleasure! What great enjoyment! I seem to myself to be already embarked.

GER. (A fine sight, that big stick impaled with that dress!)

MUS. } Set sail, row, haul, slacken.
GER. }

MUS. I am beside myself with joy.

GER. (I am beside myself with laughter.)

MUS. It seems to me I already see you in the beautiful country of Europe with French-style clothes making deep reverences when you see your Monsieur.

GER. It seems to me also I see you going gallantly around in the street with stick, hat, and sword making more reverences to me, while I say to you, "Farewell, Monsieur".

Scene xiii
ALADINO *and* ROSANA

ALA. With a good hundred wounds the traitor will by now have given up his foul soul. That crime demanded a slow death and a crueler one; but my honor and your sorrow were thirsty for too much of that blood. 109

ROS. The criminal had a quick death coming to him.

ALA. My hatred already rests calmly on the victim who has been sacrificed. Burnt offerings appease the gods. If the gods are appeased, grandees can also be appeased. If the criminals are punished, the guilt perishes with the criminals. 110

Scene xiv
ALADINO, ROSANA, *and* GERINA

GER. Ooh, madam, madam . . . 111

ROS. What news do you bring?

GER. Oh, if you only knew what treason is abroad!

ALA. What treason?

GER. Mustafà is fleeing in disguise with Ersindo and the other captives.

ROS. What do I hear?

ALA. And how? And when?

GER. Now, and he is waiting for me at the port, for in order to discover the secret I too promised to flee.

ALA. Oh, unworthy Arsace!

ROS. My king . . .

ALA. Keep silent!

ROS. (I am afraid for my brother.)

ALA. That unworthy head, which was not able to carry out my orders, shall fall at my feet. (*Exit.*)

ROS. Ah, Gerina! My brother is endangered.

GER. What did I know about Arsace? But what does it matter? With your flattery, you can easily check the king's wrath.

ROS. May Love help me in such extreme danger, and shoot his arrows from my countenance.
With a thousand and a thousand tricks may the angry ruler be appeased and caressed. An ingenious deception acquires merit and praise when it serves a great love. (*Exit.*) 112

Scene xv

Port, with illuminated ship at the shore, and other ships, also lit up, at nighttime, with the moon in the sky.

CUNEGONDA, RIDOLFO, ARSACE, ERNESTO, *and* MUSTAFÀ.

CUN. Are we safe, Ridolfo? 113

RID. Yes, my darling.

ARS. You are all already safe, and so that your well-being may be all the surer, I am coming to escort your flight.

MUS. (And Gerina is not coming?)

ERN. But to whom do we owe such precious safety?

ARS. To me, and to that deception which almost cost you your lives. Since that person is a woman, it becomes the guilt of the imprudent queen, and together with guilt all suspicion should be removed.

MUS. (And is she still not coming? I have a great fear in my heart.)

114 RID. Now that you give this foot back its precious liberty my faith promises you a suitable reward, and will give it to you.

CUN. Now that you give me back my love, which is all that this heart desires, you are a candidate for that glory which is the desire of the god of Love.

115 RID. Arsace, farewell. We shall go far away.

ARS. Halt! Before leaving, I want a pledge of your faith, that when you have returned to your kingdom, there will never be any war waged by your arms against Egypt.

RID. Ridolfo knows how to be grateful even to his enemies. I promise as much, and as a pledge of my faith and that of my Cunegonda, here is my right hand.

ARS. Thus I serve my king and myself too.

Final Scene

The same, and ALADINO, ROSANA, GERINA, *and guards with torches.*

116 ALA. What do I see? Unworthy Arsace, is this the way you serve your king and yourself?

RID. (What might this be?)

CUN. (Ah, we are lost!)

ALA. Let those wicked wretches be arrested.

ARS. Listen, O Sire. Ersindo is a woman, and a queen.

ROS. (O Heavens! What do I hear?)

ALA. Ersindo a woman?

CUN. Yes, a woman.

GER. (Now you see what a deception!)

MUS. (Crazy goings-on!)

CUN. I am Cunegonda, the heiress of Bohemia. Ridolfo is a prince, and my bridegroom. My great faithfulness was a spur to my heart to follow him, even unto fetters and death. If any pity rules in your heart, ah, do not sunder that bond which Heaven and Love have joined.

ALA. (If I did not relent, I would have the heart of a tiger.)

RID. She has her ships full of thousands of armed men. Let her head and mine fall at your feet, but await a savage revenge sooner than you expect it.

ARS. This consideration, Sire, made me disobedient to you; but I first had them swear to me eternal peace towards the sands of Africa.

ALA. (*To* ARSACE) I accept the peace, and I forgive your error.

CUN. O great-hearted soul! (Rosana, I am silent about your accusation.)

ROS. (Pardon, O Princess, an error which was the fault of Love.)

RID. Ah, the contented heart can desire no more.

ALA. In my presence let Love join your hands; and you, Rosana, extend your right hand to me, bride and queen.

RID. }
CUN. } O pleasure!

ALA. }
ROS. } O happiness!

RID. ⎫
CUN. ⎬ Let the child god join our souls.
ALA. ⎪
ROS. ⎭

ALA. Since favorable Heaven has made me worthy of such a great lot: friends, do not be unwilling to honor my wedding with your presences, and to your native shores I myself will accompany you.

RID. To such a great king, nothing can be denied. My beloved, here we are in calm.

CUN. This soul is rejoicing in my bosom for pleasure.

MUS. Since this is a day of rejoicing, my lord, please consent to my marrying Gerina.

ALA. I am willing.

GER. But first my mistress must agree.

ROS. I am willing.

MUS. Give me your hand.

GER. Here is my hand.

MUS. }
GER. } My sun, I like deeds and not words.

117 ALL After storm clouds, the sun appears joyously in heaven. Only the stars shine under the dark veil of night.

THE END